VICTORIAN FLORIDA

Overlooking Lake Worth from Palm Beach. Photograph by O. Pierre Havens, 1890.

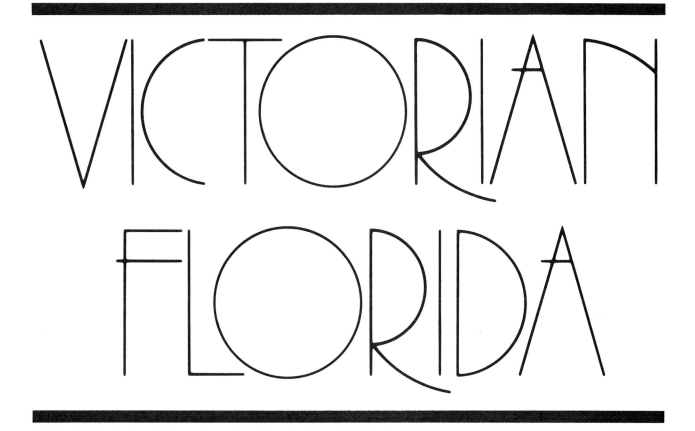

VICTORIAN FLORIDA

AMERICA'S LAST FRONTIER

FLOYD AND MARION RINHART

PEACHTREE PUBLISHERS LIMITED
Atlanta, Georgia

Published by
PEACHTREE PUBLISHERS, LTD.
494 Armour Circle, N. E.
Atlanta, Georgia 30324

Copyright © 1986 Floyd and Marion Rinhart

Manufactured in the United States of America

Design by Paulette L. Lambert

1st printing

Library of Congress Catalog Card Number: 86-61539

ISBN 0-934601-02-X

CONTENTS

ACKNOWLEDGMENTS

We are deeply indebted to our son George R. Rinhart of Colebrook, Connecticut, for his generous help in the amassing of our extensive collection of Floridana, over the years, especially of rare photographs. He has also given us access to his library, which has proven invaluable.

Special thanks should be given Jacqueline K. Bearden, St. Augustine Historical Society, who helped in locating needed research material and photographs. We are grateful to Joan Morris, Florida State Photographic Archives, Tallahassee, for allowing us to photograph from the archives collection, and also for the invaluable research materials she brought to our attention.

Other individuals and institutions helpful during our research and study or who have provided pictorial material are the following: Mike Barber, Delray Beach, Florida; Robert E. Cauthen, Leesburg, Florida; Dorothy Dodd, Tallahassee, Florida; Emerick Hanzl, Clifton, New Jersey; Dr. Robert C. Harris, Largo, Florida; Library of Congress; W. Robert Nix, Athens, Georgia; David Nolan, St. Augustine, Florida; Pinellas County Historical Museum, Largo, Florida; Bernhard C. Puckhaber, Ballston Spa, New York; St. Augustine Historical Society; and Mrs. Kenneth Woodburn, Tallahassee, Florida.

George Pierron's Photographic Studio, St. George Street, St. Augustine, copyright 1887.

According to the United States census of 1870, the state of Florida was last in the number of photographers listed—only three were documented. The census was barely complete before practitioners of the art, including Pierron, descended on the state in great numbers from all over the country, and by 1890 even the smallest of Florida towns could often boast of at least one photographer.

Florida in mid-nineteenth-century America was similar in many ways to the western frontier. Its topography was different—with lowlands, swamps, and vast bodies of water on either side of the peninsula. But the lure of wilderness yet to be explored and settled, the mysterious magnetic beckoning of the unknown, the independence of spirit brought pioneers south in search of wealth, good health, and that intangible quality—peace of mind.

Frontier Florida, after passing through Spanish and English domination and settlement, had yet another problem similar to the settling of the West, conflict with Indians. When the American military decided that the Indians must leave their lands, the Seminole Indian Wars broke out in 1835, and it was not until 1842 that an uneasy peace made Florida relatively safe. Even so, outbreaks of violence by the Indians continued into the 1850s.

The recording of Florida life and history in visual form was distinctive in that the first artist to visit the new world, Jacques De Morgues Le Moyne, a watercolorist, came to Florida with the Laudonnière expedition in 1564. He was one of the few survivors of the ill-fated Huguenot settlement on the St. Johns River destroyed by the Spanish in 1565.

Other artists came to the unspoiled frontier, notably John James Audubon, portrait and wildlife painter, who traveled along Florida's east coast and Key West in the 1830s sketching rare birds for his portfolio. George Catlin, best known for his Indian paintings, documented a way of life soon to disappear in the struggle to follow.

As with the West, photographers captured, with the camera's realistic eye, portraits of the people and scenes in a new land remote from travelers until after the Civil War. Long before photography came to America, in the fall of 1839, St. Augustine had been a haven for health seekers. And it was here where a photographer first visited Florida. Alfred A. Lansing, an artist and wood engraver from New York City, advertised in the local newspaper on April 16, 1842, as a "professor of photography" with only one minute's sitting required—the price five dollars. He also gave "Instructions in the Art." Lansing is said, by the historian Benson J. Lossing, to have been the first to engrave large pictures for circus and theatre bills.[1] His father, Garret Lansing, was one of America's earliest wood engravers. In Tallahassee, the first recorded daguerreotypist, Andrew Scott, advertised in January of 1843. As time went on, a number of daguerreotypists, as early photographers were called, migrated from other Southern states to the busy state capital.

In 1844, H. Whittemore, a New Orleans daguerreotypist, came to Apalachicola, a busy port town in the northwest part of the state. During the next few years he took views of the West Indies and Florida, and in 1851 exhibited forty views at the American Institute, New York City, which included two of Florida—one of the Cotton Landing in Apalachicola and the other of Key West. Whittemore was made an offer for his collection by a well-known illustrated London newspaper, but it is not known whether the offer was accepted.

Another daguerreotypist, Nathan S.

Southern Gems.

By the Florida Club.

Bennett, from Washington, D.C., took a portrait of the "Florida Warrior Billy Bow Legs," and in 1853, according to *Humphrey's Journal*, a photographic publication, he was injured on board the steamer *Empire* and lost a valuable collection of daguerreotypes.

Unfortunately, many valuable daguerreotypes suffered a similar fate, and Florida's history will not be complete until the lives of these early artists and their work are fully rediscovered.

During the 1850s photographs on glass, paper, and sheet iron gradually began replacing the old daguerreotype, an image mirrored on a silvered-copper plate. The parlor stereoscope, introduced to America in 1852, was an ornate apparatus which enabled the viewer to see, through twin magnifying glasses, two photographs mounted side by side, which blended into a single three-dimensional picture. Quickly improved by the Americans, a variety of table models was soon available to the public. At first daguerreotypes and ambrotypes (photographs on glass) were used in the viewers, but by the mid-1850s paper stereo prints, mounted on cardboard, gained a measure of popularity. However, after Oliver Wendell Holmes invented a simple hand stereo viewer in 1859, stereographs became a national mania. Almost overnight, they could be found in the parlor of the most humble home.

Edward Anthony and Company of New York, the country's largest photographic supply house, quickly became involved in America's new pastime and soon found a large market for scenes of both European and American life and scenery. An advertisement appeared in a St. Augustine newspaper in early 1860 for revolving stereoscopes which could show from twelve to one hundred scenes. Also offered were Instantaneous Views of Europe and America. The company was also prepared to outfit amateur photographers with all necessary instruction and equipment to take stereoscopic pictures. They advised that they wanted first class stereoscopic negatives: "Send by

The Old Spanish Lighthouse, St. Augustine, c. 1870. Stereograph by the Florida Club.

"…a weather beaten tower standing almost in the water, regularly fortified with walls, angles, and loopholes—a lovely little stronghold down by the sea. It was a picturesque old beacon, built by the Spaniards a long time ago as a look-out; when the English came into possession of Florida, in 1763, they raised the look-out sixty feet higher, and planted a cannon on the top, to be fired as a signal when a vessel came in sight…in old times a bonfire was lighted on top every night." (From *Harper's New Monthly Magazine*, 1874.) The old lighthouse was swept out to sea in 1879.

mail a print unmounted, with price of negative," a notice important to Florida's visual history because it indicates the demand for views and the competitive prices. It is interesting that negatives were bought from other than Anthony's own photographers. The fact is that some of the finest stereoscopic views of Florida life and scenery were published by E. Anthony & Company and by E. & H.T. Anthony (a partnership between Edward and his brother).

The paper stereograph was a popular money-making item with photographers. Views of summer and winter resorts were especially in demand and sold well in hotels, bookstores, and novelty shops; they could also be ordered by mail from catalogs issued by the large supply houses.

During the Civil War, travel in Florida was stagnant. Few photographers, with the exception of the military, made photographs. Sam A. Cooley, the famous army photographer, "secured photographs at Jacksonville, [and] St. Augustine." And the famous Civil War artist and illustrator Alfred R. Waud, best known for his illustrations in *Harper's Weekly*, sketched a few scenes of Florida.

After the Civil War and until the turn of the century, some of America's finest photographers came to Florida, and they not only recorded in photographs stereo views for parlor viewing but made superb large prints, works of art in their delicate plays of light and shade.

The Anthony Company sent their foremost photographer, Thomas C. Roche, on a Southern tour, which included Florida, in the fall of 1873. He took views of Charleston, Savannah, Jacksonville, and

"Crackers on the Move." De Funiak Springs, c. 1889.

The advertisement on the building was for W.B. Shear & J. Flournoy, photographers.

scenes along the St. Johns and Ocklawaha rivers. Roche had won great admiration from the viewing public with his magnificent scenes of Yosemite taken in 1870-1871. Other famous photographers, George Barker and Charles Bierstadt, both from Niagara Falls, came at different times to secure images of Florida to bring back home. In 1856 the famous pioneer western photographer Benjamin Franklin Upton, who had emigrated from Maine to Minnesota, photographed Indian tribes—the Sioux, Chippewa, and Winnebago, Mississippi shipping, and other scenes of the West. He moved to St. Augustine in 1875 because of his wife's health. An artist with a camera, he became the pioneer photographer of Florida, taking landscape views for over twenty years.

During the 1880s most large towns and cities in Florida had one or more pho-tographers. Some of these became well-known landscape artists and were commissioned to make views which were used in the widespread promotion of Florida for both tourism and land sales. For example, the well-known photographer of the West, Stanley J. Morrow, came to Florida in about 1882 and worked for the South Publishing Company, which put out the illustrated Plant Railroad System booklets.

Promoters also publicized Florida in England. Transparencies made from photographs of northern Florida, taken in 1886 by Horace Warren Gridley, were projected on the screen in the Exhibition Hall of the Photographic Society of Great Britain. Represented were Florida pines, live oaks, palmettos, and other vegetation, wagon travel, and what was said to be the gem of them all, "a lady on horseback

P.J. Crawford, Gallery (and wife), Fort Meade, c. 1890.

An old-time upstairs studio. When American commercial photography began in 1840, daguerreotypists often displayed their pictures at the entrance to the studio—a tradition followed by Crawford some fifty years later.

10

defiling through a pass amid trunks and branches of trees."

The number of English photographers who came to America in the nineteenth century is unknown, but one of the most famous English photographic historians, J. Traill Taylor, owned a picturesque estate called Nirthsdale in Lane Park, near Tavares. Taylor had been a contributor to the *British Journal of Photography* from 1859 and was the editor of the famous publication from 1864-1879. He edited the New York *Photographic Times* from 1880-1885. From 1886 until his death in 1895, he once again edited the prestigious *British Journal of Photography*.

Florida also beckoned naturalists and scientists with cameras in the 1880s. One party left Barnstable, Massachusetts, by sea, arriving at New Smyrna after a tedious passage of twenty-five days, their object being to explore Lake Okeechobee. They brought photographic apparatus with one hundred negatives and a stock of artists' supplies. Natural history specimens and Indian relics were to be collected for the Smithsonian and other scientific institutions.

One of America's leading landscape photographers, O. Pierre Havens, left Savannah, Georgia, in 1888 for Jacksonville, where he would become, in the next fifteen years, the leading photographer in the state. Also appearing on the Florida scene in the late 1880s, and again in the early 1890s, was the most famous photographer of the West, William Henry Jackson, of Denver, Colorado. His first trip took him along the Indian and the St. Johns rivers, then on to St. Augustine. During the second trip he took photographs of the Royal Poinciana at Palm Beach and also took extensive pictures of the Ponce de Leon Hotel in St. Augustine. Jackson concentrated particularly on the hotel's ornate ceilings and produced some of his best work. A St. Augustine newspaper item on March 1, 1891, stated that Jackson's photographs were to be

Posing the subject. Alvin Harper Studio, Tallahassee, c. 1885.

found at El Unico, a shop under the arch of the Hotel Cordova: "Beauties of St. Augustine and tropical scenery of Florida reproduced with photographic accuracy, while the brush of the artist has so well supplemented the work of the camera that the pictures have the effect of being photographed in colors. Jackson's photographs are known everywhere as the best. His Florida views are sold only at El Unico."

O. Pierre Havens, Jacksonville, c. 1894.

By the time Havens opened a studio in Jacksonville in 1888, his artistic handling of light and shade had gained him national recognition as one of the best photographers of his time. Flagler used many of Haven's photographs to illustrate the Florida East Coast Railroad brochures.

Artists also came to St. Augustine in the late 1880s, after Flagler had built his fabulous hotels. In the rear of the Ponce de Leon Hotel were studios occupied by well-known painters, including the famous Martin J. Heade, landscape artist.

St. Augustine was also a headquarters for amateur photographers, especially late in the century. A local publication, *The Tatler*, sponsored contests for the best photographs, and all visitors to the east coast of Florida could compete. The most prominent of the amateurs taking photographs in Florida was Leonard Dakin, a banker from New York State, who came in hope of recovering his health in the mid-1880s. His father owned a large orange grove near Georgetown, on the St. Johns River, and during his few years on the plantation, Dakin made photographs of Florida life.

Another amateur photographer, who took very rare photographs of Dry Tortugas and Key West, was Dr. Joseph Bassett Holder, surgeon, zoologist, and author, who was the surgeon-in-charge of the United States military prison in Tortugas from 1860-1867, during the historical period of the Civil War when Dr. Samuel A. Mudd and other conspirators were sent to Tortugas after the Lincoln assassination.

In the winter of 1896, a professional photographer from Ballston Spa, New York, made a unique photographic record of his trip to Florida. He created the first complete stereopticon slide lecture series about the state of Florida. Jesse S. Wooley became an expert in the use of stereopticon (dissolving views) when he worked as a partner, from 1893, with the famous photographer Seneca Ray Stoddard, of Glen Falls, New York, who was known as the "Mathew Brady" of the North country, and an expert in the field of tourist promotion.

The rare illustrations chosen for this book from hundreds of old photographs represent an excellent cross section of Florida. They are derived from stereographs, paper prints, tintypes, and photogravures, with a few sketches and engravings added for interest. All photographs have been dated using our extensive knowledge in the history of American nineteenth-century photography, and we have correlated, through research, the background of each scene as closely as possible to make the particular time element come alive. Selected from a wide range of subjects, these images best illustrate Florida through the eyes of the Victorian tourist. ■

Jesse Sumner Wooley, Ballston Spa, New York, c. 1903.

Wooley was the first photographer to give a lecture travelogue of Florida, illustrated with photographic slides reproduced from photographs taken on his tour of the state in 1896.

"The Hammock," Palatka, c. 1890. Photograph attributed to William H. Jackson.

A Southern railroad engine and crew awaiting next assignment, c. 1874.

It was necessary to ride on a number of cooperating but independently owned railroads to reach Florida from New York. A Pullman traveler, enclosed in a through car, was often unaware when the next railroad line and a new engine and crew had taken over the train's operation.

Traveling South

The nineteenth century was a period of rapid change, of almost constant upheaval in the nation's way of life, including modes of travel. In the 1830s, new marvels in boat and rail transportation abruptly appeared, and paddle-wheel steamers became commonplace on America's lakes and rivers. The age of steam was making a noisy entrance. By 1840, the chug of a locomotive was no longer a strange and unfamiliar sound as ribbons of steel began linking towns and cities. As travel to Europe improved, the five-week sailing packet became outdated. The changing sea lanes now saw three British steamships plying between England and New York in fourteen days. Speed became a national mania with Americans, and newspapers provided eager readers with accounts of daring deeds and mishaps encountered by boat and rail.

In the 1840s, with the Seminole Indians in full flight and statehood a reality, Florida was ready for its first flood of health seekers. Frontier explorers in Florida called the newcomers "winter tourists." The Eastern watering places of Cape May, Newport, Saratoga, and Long Branch—the ultimate dictators in summer resort fashion—would have, within a few years, a wintertime counterpart.

Prior to the 1840s, a trip to Florida was an adventuresome and often hazardous experience aboard an itinerant sailing vessel running from New York to Charleston or Savannah, whose zigzag schedule could exasperate the most patient of travelers. Then too there was the danger of passing stormy Cape Hatteras and the inevitable bout with seasickness, a tariff old Neptune generally demanded. Land travel was still less inviting aboard a jolting stage coach with an independent driver, a journey which did little to improve one's health or disposition.

The dreary old four-to-eight-day sailing trip was replaced in the 1840s by ocean-going steamships and coastal steamers. However, a few stubborn invalids still preferred the slow sea voyage, declaring that it was beneficial to their health, regardless of *mal de mer*.

In the fall of 1842, a timetable trip from New York to Palatka became a reality. The last link in the steam route to Florida had its beginning in November when the steamer *St. Matthews* initiated weekly service between Savannah and Palatka, with ports of call along the route.

By the 1842-43 winter season, a tourist could take the "cars" from New York to Baltimore, then board a Chesapeake Bay steamer to Portsmouth, where the cars were again boarded to bring the traveler directly to Wilmington, North Carolina, with only one transfer at Weldon. A fast "rail-boat" side-wheeler connected Wilmington with Charleston and Savannah. Fare on the new steam route from New York to Savannah was fifty dollars, about double the price for the old sailing packet.

Palmetto Thatch Shed, Sketched by Alfred R. Waud, c. 1865.

"When the first frost paints, with singular fidelity, a Florida hammock on the window pane, the invalid and tourist searches his maps to learn some more about Florida."

Florida. Palmetto thatch shed

The Pavilion Hotel, Savannah, c. 1870. Photograph by Jerome N. Wilson.

Well recommended by tourists—"A quiet pleasant house, $3.00 per day."

Savannah, a picturesque and hospitable little town, fitted perfectly into the Northern notion of Southern life, offering even slavery for the wide-eyed Yankee. Tourists could walk the many shady parks and squares and perhaps tarry briefly by unique aboveground burial tombs. The bustle of city life was left far behind in the easygoing Southern port.

Despite the danger of an occasional Indian arrow and delays encountered in crossing shallow bars on the inland water route, the *St. Matthews*, plying between Savannah and Palatka, became a financial success; a second steamer, *William Gaston*, added to the line in 1845, provided semi-weekly service. Both were designated U.S. Mail Steamers. Tourists and settlers came south in ever-increasing numbers, and in 1848 boat passage between Palatka and Enterprise began, bringing passengers halfway down the Florida peninsula to Lake Monroe, as yet a frontier wilderness.

America enjoyed a period of great prosperity in the 1850s, and the Florida trade, like the nation, prospered. By the end of the decade, a number of propeller-driven

The *Florence*, May, 1871. Photograph by E. & H.T. Anthony.

The pirated St. Johns, Florida, steamer at a Savannah wharf after its recapture. The ship had been stolen at Jacksonville and seized along the Georgia coast by a U.S. revenue cutter.

steamships ran regularly between Savannah and New York, Philadelphia, and Boston—swift ships that travelers much preferred over the little-improved southbound railroads. Meanwhile, the *St. Matthews* and *William Gaston* had competition from two large palatial steamers, the *St. Marys* and the *St. Johns* (equal in size and appointments to the famous Hudson River steamers) plying between Savannah and Palatka. The link southward from Palatka had also changed in the early 1850s with the steamers *Darlington* and *Barnet* carrying more and more tourists to Enterprise.

During the Civil War years in Florida, for both tourist and settler, time stood still. The Savannah and St. Johns river steamers temporarily disappeared, some commandeered, others moved elsewhere. When peace returned, tourists once again streamed to the nation's winter playground. Florida during this era might be likened to the American West, a wilderness waiting exploration. Aware of the new exodus from the North, the steamship companies now looked for additional fertile fields of revenue.

By the winter season of 1869-70, the Savannah-Palatka water route flourished once again. The old *St. Matthews* line had converted to luxury steamers—the *Lizzie Baker* and the *Nick King*. Also the New York City commuter-steamer *Sylvan Shore* was sent south for the season for the run between Savannah and Fernandina. A tourist guidebook for 1869 suggested: "To go quickly and comfortably—go by rail to Charleston and take a steamer among the islands that line the coast." Although Savannah remained the favorite port for Florida travel, many tourists liked to make a stopover at historic Charleston, where passage could be taken directly to Palatka on the large steamers *Dictator* and *City Point*.

Beneath the palmetto or enjoying the climate. Savannah, c. 1871. Photograph by Jerome N. Wilson.

Saloon of steamer *St. Johns*, c. 1867. Photograph by E. Anthony.

Luxurious comfort for travelers between Savannah and the towns along the St. Johns River.

If ship lines were reaping a harvest in revenues between Charleston, Savannah, and Florida, not so the railroads. As primitive as ten years before, the Savannah-Jacksonville train still took sixteen hours to make the run via Live Oak and Baldwin.

Nor would change come by 1876, when an intrepid Bostonian insisted that he would travel all the way to Jacksonville by rail. In recounting his journey, he found no fault with the link between Boston and Washington. However, after the train left Washington at midnight, he observed: "Even the sleeping-car (and may I never rest in my coffin, if it is any narrower than the berths in the sleeping car which takes us southward out of Washington!) fails to take the romance out.... In point of fact we are approaching Petersburg. I draw aside the dingy little window curtain, poke away my book which has kept the window open...and lying at ease in my coffin, watch with all enthusiasm my first sunrise in the South." After breakfast, he commented: "Nobody would eat in Weldon who hadn't waited three hours for breakfast.... Everything tastes like everything else and everything tastes fried.... Never did a railroad train jog like ours—the lassitude of the South has crept into the very cog-wheels and the smoke stack itself breathes wearily."[1]

When the Bostonian reached Savannah, he saw an old lady screaming because the horses ran away with the omnibus. He writes: "My winter cloak and I parted company at Savannah.... It is warm, warm. I envy the lady in the linen duster.... Jacksonville looks like Lowell on a July day."[2]

For the wealthy traveler things had

Pullman accommodations, c. 1879.

been quite different two years earlier when the first Florida-bound private rail car left Jersey City on February 26, 1874, at 9 A.M. A gay and noisy party was aboard—a mayor, a banker, railroad presidents, an editor, a merchant, a lawyer, and their wives. The car named *Pennsylvania* was a sixty-three-foot, twelve-wheel ornate wonder, painted maroon with contrasting brown undercarriage and green wheels. The graceful, pointed gothic windows hinted at an elegant interior. The car featured three large rooms: a kitchen with pantries, refrigerator, cooking range, hot and cold water; a well-furnished parlor; and a dining room replete with India china and choice linens. Both rooms converted into sleeping apartments, including a ladies' dressing room. The bathroom, besides the usual appointments, contained a bathtub, a first in rail travel. An electric call bell sounded between the rooms. The rear observation deck, decorated with a shining brass rail, was large enough to hold ten chairs, a pleasurable feature, especially during the evening hours.

Pullman Palace Car, c. 1878. Photograph by H. Ropes & Co., New York.

The "Drawing Room" car, with its easy chairs, was considered by most travelers well worth the extra cost for comfortable travel during daylight hours.

"Pouring the Champagne." From a railroad booklet, c. 1880.

Elaborate meals aboard the *Chicago Limited* in the early 1880s were one dollar. A quart of imported chilled champagne was three dollars extra.

As the "little hotel rolled away southward," the entertainment began. One of the party observed: "A marked feature of the first day was dinner. The household was too numerous for the table and gallantry prompted the gentlemen to insist the ladies should dine first…an experiment not repeated."[3] It seemed that the women had anticipated or at least expected an invitation back into the dining room after the men had finished their repast. "But," he adds, "they were barred out. In vain they implored admission to that festive board. They stood without the closed door and heard the 'sounds of revelry,' and exhausted all their arguments and entreaties upon…the master of the feast. He was obdurate. His jolly companions greeted the lamentations of the outsiders with roars of laughter. And he would occasionally open the door and roll out an empty bottle."[4] The trip was off to a good start!

At bedtime, another question was raised—who would sleep where? The story continues: "A Pullman car was attached to the train and places enough engaged for those who could not sleep in our car, which accommodates only eight sleepers. The gentlemen magnanimously offered to keep our own car and surrender the Pullman places to the ladies. The ladies learned enough that night to know that their travelling hotel was better than any of the Pullman palaces. And when they crept out of their holes in the morning, after being entertained with the clanging noise of gauge adjustments at midnight, at Greensboro, they presented a striking contrast to the hilarious dinner party of the preceding day."[5]

Meanwhile, steamship lines running from northern ports continued to prosper. From 1877 the popular Mallory Line, for example, had a weekly three-and-a-half-day run from New York to Fernandina, stopping at Charleston along the way. The famous Clyde Line, new in 1886, began the first direct service from New

From an advertisement in *Harper's Monthly Magazine*, 1881.

The Mallory Steamship Line advertisement. From the Savannah city directory, 1877.

York to Jacksonville. By the 1890s three Clyde Liners departed New York for Florida each week.

Winds of change were evident by 1880, when railroad promoters suddenly realized that they had been looking westward while missing a lucrative southern market.

The winter season of 1881-82 opened with the railroads advertising their Florida route as the most convenient and comfortable: "Railroad facilities from all northern points to Florida have greatly changed in the past year, and vexations, delays, uncertain connections, slow trains, inattention and general discomforts experienced by travelers during

"Moss-draped trees and warm days." Southern railroad scenery, c. 1885. Photograph by William H. Jackson.

A view of old plantation life, c. 1879. Photograph by J.A. Palmer.

recent seasons are happily ended."[6] The answer to the railroad's problem had been to build a junction point at Waycross, Georgia, where lines would converge from all over the country.

Throughout the 1880s, an intense rivalry began between rail and ship routes, making the tourist a pampered object of travel lore. A Florida railroad booklet for 1887 promised an earthly paradise: "Soft cushioned divans receive his body; a delicate luncheon is served at any hour; an airy 'smoker' invites him to gossip with his fellow guests—they cannot be travelers. No, he is a guest of a hotel on wings. The grain of polished wood and nickel mountings, and mirrors reflect the flying scene without, strengthens the self deception. Towns, stations, villages are flushed like partridge and go whirling out of sight…. With hoarse throttle valve bellowing, we cross the iron bridge over the Savannah River. But why loiter over charming local resorts when Florida beckons with its coy retreats and lovely byplaces that fashion seeks when dumb-frost paints its mark on the window pane."[7]

The Florida-bound railroads widened their appeal to those of social standing by introducing the extra-fare all-Pullman express. Many had names similar to the Pennsylvania Railroad's New York to Chicago *Broadway Limited*, a legend for luxury in the 1880s. Probably the best known of the deluxe trains was the Florida East Coast's *Florida and West Indies Limited*, only thirty-six hours from New York. The Southern Railroad ran the *New York and Florida Express* and the *Great Cincinnati and Florida Express*. The Seaboard's New York trains and *The Limited* and *The Dixie Flyer* from St. Louis also catered to those seeking the luxury ride south. The elite rode in high style. More than twenty private cars a day cleared Jacksonville each winter season in the 1890s.

Timetable, New York to Florida, 1884-1885 season.

The Clyde Liner *Algonquin* at Pier 29 beneath the Brooklyn Bridge, near departure time, 3 P.M. on January 27, 1896. Photograph by Jesse S. Wooley.

Hints to Travelers

After the Civil War, when travel to faraway places once again beckoned the tourist, guide books for all areas of the country became popular items for those wishing to extend their horizons beyond an everyday, humdrum existence. Descriptive books about Florida were especially in demand. Invalids or those who wished to avoid the rigors of winter whiled away hours reading about an easier life in the tropics. These books gave practical advice on how to prepare for the journey, what to bring and what not to bring, and how to eliminate or keep to a minimum the many unforeseen pitfalls along the way. Informative details about climate, transportation, and locales of the state made possible the planning of a satisfactory itinerary in a strange new land.

Dr. Daniel Brinton's guide book of 1869 suggested a visit to the dentist as a necessary precaution, for what could be worse than a "jumping toothache" along the way when a pleasant journey was anticipated. Soap, brushes, and other companion articles essential for grooming had best be handy, and extra towels were deemed a necessity in many areas of the South, because otherwise the local vegetation might have to do. Brinton advised "tinted spectacles," one or two air-cushions, and a pair of easy slippers as comforting items for weary travelers. Above all, he advised bringing a silk mosquito net, insect repellent, a pocket knife, and a strong umbrella. Also, a few local histories and maps close at hand would give the traveler a quick reference at each stop along the way.

A southbound tourist was advised to do without the companionship of a dog. An article in *Lippincott's Magazine* of 1870 advised: "You had better not take a dog, unless you dislike him and want to lose him: he will feed the first alligator you meet in fording a stream."

As to clothing, flannel underwear was recommended for winter days. However,

Typical tourists, c. 1883. Because of alligators, tourists were advised to leave their dogs at home.

Dr. Brinton found the popular rubber overcoats, rubber boots, and overshoes objectionable outerwear for invalids. For proper headgear en route, a hood was recommended for the ladies, a soft felt hat for men. The best shoes for travel were double-soled, low with broad heels, "laced firmly around the ankle, and fitted loosely over the toes."

Charles Norton's 1890 guide book advised woolen undergarments, shirts, and hosiery of light or medium thickness, camel's hair and unshrinkable flannels being preferred. If a traveler with limited

Driving through the pine barrens, c. 1890.

Riding was advised along the sandy roads. Walking trips were discouraged except for beach areas where the sand was firm. On day excursions it was recommended that an insect repellent be taken as a precaution against the powerful "red bug," mosquitoes, or other pests.

A rowboat at Silver Springs, c. 1877.

A sturdy umbrella was a necessity for the tourists. It provided protection from the sun or rain. Straw hats were advised for warm days; soft felt hats for cooler weather.

baggage found it inconvenient to carry a full supply of thick underwear for sudden drops in temperature, Norton suggested donning two suits of light underwear at once! Another alternative would be to purchase necessary items in Florida at prices higher than in New York. Soft felt hats were recommended as good cool weather items, and for warmer days, straw and palmetto hats could be purchased in Jacksonville or St. Augustine. As trains were notoriously dusty, long cloaks called dusters gave sensible protection, although they were unstylish and unbecoming to the wearer.

In a horse-loving age, the needs of the equestrian were always considered. Good saddle horses could be obtained at reasonable prices in almost any area of Florida. Riding through the woods and along the beaches was considered both enjoyable and healthful, especially for the consumptives and invalids who made up a great portion of Southern tourists in the nineteenth century.

However, although riding was recommended, walking trips were discouraged because of the great distances between Florida towns. Also, the sandy country roads made walking tiresome. If pedestrians did hike through the tangled Florida scrub, they had best heed the warning about the tiny but powerful "red bug," which, once entrenched under the skin, gave the victim many days of itching and discomfort. For such hikes, high boots or tight leggings in leather or canvas gave some protection against the pests.

All in all, the tourists managed very well despite innumerable complaints. Once in the land of sunshine all was forgotten, and even poor accommodations could be taken in stride when warm balmy days could be spent outdoors. Nature took over to soothe the most irritable disposition.

The Sportsmen

Nothing promised greater adventure to nineteenth-century sportsmen than a winter's sojourn into the Florida wilderness. An excursion party required one or two boats, camping equipment, and ample provisions. Careful planning was of utmost importance because few luxuries would be waiting in Florida.

Before leaving New York, some choice items were bought: prime coffee, English teas, and other foods for the epicurean. It was not an unusual sight in midwinter to see a man entering a Broadway shop to ask for "four yards of silk tissue." The saleswoman would nod and say: "Yes, sir; veils. For Florida? We sell this veiling every day in winter. Take it green. It's more becoming and comfortable for the eyes. No mosquito can get through it."[8]

Lunch time, camping out. St. Johns Island, c. 1875. Photograph by J.F. Mears.

**Alligator party, 1870.
Photograph by A.F. Styles.**

Some sportsmen shipped their boats, tents, and other supplies aboard a sailing vessel or steamer several weeks in advance of sailing to Savannah or Jacksonville, or to Cedar Keys or Manatee on Florida's west coast. Other excursion parties chose to charter or buy a boat on arrival.

For the west coast waters, an ideal craft was a flat-bottomed schooner. Water storage was important, and a good supply of canned meat was considered an essential part of the grocery list. Also, the sportsman needed guns, ammunition, fishing tackle, an axe, a spade, a hatchet, cooking utensils, a tent, a lantern, candles, and innumerable other items for outdoor camp life.

The usual excursion party hired guides and a cook, and work both aboard ship and in camp was divided among the group. Plentiful game and fish usually provided "meat for the pot." However, by the 1870s, game was regulated and controlled by many laws, so it was best that sportsmen have emergency food supplies.

Returning homeward, bronze and pocked with mosquito bites, the sportsman brought with him unforgettable memories of soft tropical winds, clear waters teaming with wildlife, myriads of colorful birds, and brilliant sunsets. The hunting had become incidental.

Climate and Accommodations

Although not many Americans read the *American Journal of Science and Arts* in 1839, its articles were often reprinted because they were considered beyond reproach. During the year, an article appeared based on the diary of Major Henry Whiting, and his words were a prophetic vision of Florida: "The climate of Florida during the six or seven months from October is truly delicious. The frosts are few and slight, leaving vegetation its verdue and flowers their bloom throughout the year." He also stated: "Invalids have long looked to Florida as a refuge from the Northern winter, and during the disturbances of the last few years, St. Augustine has necessarily been the only place of resort. But when peace shall be established and the St. Johns re-occupied, that river will present many places of great attraction to the infirm and pulmonic."[9]

The prophecy came true more quickly than expected. The St. Johns River became popular with tourists in the 1840s. One tourist, wintering in Savannah, took the inland passage to Palatka, the site of a military post, for a three-week

Welles House, Palatka, February, 1874.

Typical of a first-class boarding house of the mid-1870s.

stay, arriving on January 3, 1843. The boarding house where he roomed was much better than expected, although he complained: "It is like many of the Southern Houses without lath or plaster...as the carpenters now [are] not particular about matching thin boards, and have no use for windows, the chinks being large enough to let in the light of day, as well as the houses of heaven."[10]

After the Civil War, thrifty Northerners, especially New Englanders, invested in land and began building boarding houses and small hotels for the winter trade. Meanwhile, land promoters, hoping to catch the unwary newcomers, built small hotels in strategic areas, which served as headquarters for their operations.

By 1870 the new innkeepers were under fire from irate tourists: "It is best to

"Coming from the station." Palatka, c. 1878. Photograph attributed to C. Seaver, Jr.

If the steamer landing or railroad station were within five miles of a town, a wagon trip would usually cost twenty-five cents per person and the same amount for each piece of luggage.

avoid the towns, however, especially the hotels. Florida innkeepers are generally sharks...and charge you double price for what they do not furnish once."[11] All agreed that the best hotels and boarding houses were kept by Vermonters!

Most tourists came from the great cities and villages of the North, and the greatest outpouring was during the last two weeks of February and the first two weeks of March. Hotels and boarding houses were taxed to overflowing, and some tourists, on hearing the discouraging news in Charleston or Savannah, returned home or stayed in other areas of the South.

By the mid-1870s many visitors came earlier. Hotels did a brisk business in November, and most were open, with the exception of a few larger ones catering to the carriage trade. The average board at a

"Hurry up there, we can't wait." Typical country outhouse, c. 1889.

Jacksonville hotel in 1875 did not advance over the previous year, but because of its popularity as a resort, rents were higher for a good furnished room, without board—never less than twenty-five to forty dollars a month. A newspaper correspondent recounted: "There is no such thing as cheap board in any desirable location in Florida. With the exception of rents the cost of living is not high."[12] Visitors of moderate means sought cheaper accommodations along the St. Johns River or in the interior regions. As time went on, invalids were discouraged by most hotel owners; the pitiful sights they presented were not conducive to moneymaking.

In the wilder regions of Florida, the tourist still depended upon the local "crackers" for hospitality. A Connecticut Yankee told of his experience along the Ocklawaha River: "We were met at a landing up the Ocklawaha by a cracker named Jim Blood.... Two of us occupied a thing called a bed, raised on some rived boards a few inches above the floor, and the other two bunked on their blankets on the floor itself, and this so filled the room that we were compelled to put our clothes outside on the piazza. A cross-cut saw was

balanced across a pole over our heads... suggesting unpleasant things.... Hard spots in our bolster were due to buttons on children's clothing... and when we arose in the morning we found them outside waiting for their garments. The same steamer that brought us had also brought Mrs. B two tin bake pans, and these were given us for wash-basins.... We used our vests for towels." Breakfast consisted of something fried, but the travelers could not tell what it was. In a curious fashion, one teaspoon circulated about the table, and the meal was enlivened by the presence of a flea-abounding pig. The host explained, "that yer pig had been brought up just like the children."[13]

A shack along the Ocklawaha River, c. 1878. Photograph by Alonzo G. Grant.

Sportsmen, if traveling by steamer, often stayed overnight in native cabins along the river where accommodations were unbelievably crude.

Cracker and wife, c. 1872. Photograph by J.A. Palmer.

Entrance, Ponce de Leon Hotel, St. Augustine, 1890. Photograph by Upton and Havens.

"The entrance court is a veritable tropical garden, with fountain and electric illumination, and on three sides rise the broken outlines of the soft blue-gray walls, lighted by the mellow terra cotta trimmings and the rich red of the crinkled roof-tiles, while across the fourth extends the covered portico—a favorite resort of smokers—with its massive gateway in the center. 'Bien Venito' twinkles in colored electric lights on the entrance. The material everywhere is a shell concrete made from the native coquina." (From *Demorest's Family Magazine*, 1893.)

Along with primitive accommodations came the inevitable outhouses. An Englishman staying at a villa in Jacksonville in the mid-1880s wrote of an outbuilding located at the end of a wooden pier extending out a little way into the river. He recounted that it was replete with noxious insects, including a mammoth spider waiting just over the threshold; also he found the dried specimens on the many webs fascinating in their variety.

In contrast to this relatively simple and carefree mode of life were the palatial hotels to come in the late 1880s and 1890s. When Henry Flagler, the great railroad entrepreneur, chose St. Augustine to promote a group of magnificent hotels, he perhaps unknowingly took the first step in solidifying Florida's east coast for future tourism. The beauties and richness of the Spanish architecture Flagler chose for his hotel ventures—the colorful tiles, spacious courtyards, and the exotic foliage—charmed the beholder.

One party staying at St. Augustine's Ponce de Leon Hotel, paid seventy-five dollars a day for three bedrooms, a bathroom, and a parlor—a unit which took up a corner of the ground floor. Another woman and her maid paid thirty-nine dollars a day for room and meals. Of course, the hotel bill did not include tips for the headwaiter, waiters, bellboys, ice-water boy, and bootblack.

By the mid-1890s, when rail travel reached south Florida, other ornate hotels followed and a new era for tourism began. By the close of the nineteenth century, the early problems of tourist accommodations had been overcome. Florida had become the winter playground of America. ■

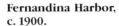

Fernandina Harbor,
c. 1900.

Map of Florida, 1860.

Once the tourist reached Savannah, he could plan his Florida campaign, as steamboat and railroad lines from all parts of the country were concentrated here. By 1870 there were two ways of reaching Jacksonville—by night train or by steamboat, which called for inland travel most of the way. However, passengers were warned of running aground and remaining on board the vessel for a week!

On a showery February morning of 1870, one traveler chose the little steamer *Nick King* for the journey. After the boat ventured out into Sapelo Sound, the sun came up and a fresh wind blew— "a glorious sight, such as makes the artist's heart ache with despair that then and there he can not fix the fleeting vision upon enduring canvas." The next morning the little steamer touched at Brunswick, Georgia, and arrived at St. Mary's, one of the most ancient settlements on the continent, later that day. Near nightfall, the steamer reached Fernandina, but because of a storm, the passengers had to remain on the island all night and all the next day, which gave them an opportunity to explore the magnificent beach.

Although most visitors found the old town charming, one tourist arriving by steamer at 5 A.M. complained: "It was low tide; and the wharf had a kind of black-spider look, which did not charm, neither did it deter us from dressing, and proceeding on shore. The wharf is a projecting one, with a commodious warehouse at the landing....A brief excursion satisfied us that this was an uninviting place to stay in. Its look of decay and hard times seemed as legible as if written on every plank in town."[1]

Amelia Island, the site of Fernandina, was rich in historical memories. Of interest to tourists were tales of smuggling operations on the island early in the century. After the Civil War, the town found favor once again as a winter and summer resort.

A tourist of 1878 described the town as being divided into old and new Fernandina: "The former...is a curious, sleepy hamlet, occupied chiefly by pilots....The new town of Fernandina...is to all intents and purposes a place of recent growth."[2] The new settlement was laid out on the former eighteenth-century plantation of

the noble English house of Egmont. Visitors were impressed with the charming residences and well-kept streets, shaded with great live oaks, magnolias, and other evergreens. Gardens were colorful with brilliant flowering shrubs and luxuriant rose bushes. The town had two hospitable hotels, the Riddle House and the Norwood House, and by 1880 the Egmont, one of the finest in the South, had been built.

North Florida surf with a storm approaching, c. 1898.

Fort Clinch, Fernandina, c. 1900.

The fort was named after General Duncan L. Clinch (1787-1849), Southern hero of the Seminole Wars and owner of a plantation near St. Marys, Georgia.

Not only was Fernandina an agreeable and salubrious resort, but it had rare attractions to yachtsmen and sportsmen. The wide expanse of Cumberland Sound and its many interesting inlets offered unlimited opportunities for cruising. The beautiful Cumberland Island on the coast of Georgia, long a resort for artists, sportsmen, and tourists, made a pleasant daytime excursion. Of special interest to visitors was Dungeness, the old crumbling estate of General Nathaniel Greene of Revolutionary War fame.

The most popular feature of Amelia Island was the beach: "On the sea side is a continuous beach fifteen miles long, broad, hard, white, and smooth as a floor. On one side is the ever-rolling surf, on the other are the low, abrupt cliffs, fringed with long salt-grass, and here and there a scrubby palmetto. Worm-eaten logs, bits of wreck, and battered hulks break the monotony of such a stretch of sand, and countless sea-birds, snipe, cranes, curlew, plover, and teal, dot the glistening beach. No finer race-course can be found. When the moon rises, at the full, above the sea, the scene is superb."[3]

During the 1890s Amelia Beach was the summer gathering place for people from nearby states. Unlike Northern resorts, no fashionable bathing hour was decreed, and the women's bathing costumes were not the suggestive abbreviations of Narragansett or Atlantic City but retained the old modesty of their grandmothers.

Late in the afternoon, riding parties of young people gathered along the beach. Wiry little Texas ponies and "Tackies" were used for both riding and driving, and carriages were mostly the ever-popular "buggies." The victorias or barouches had an antebellum air, and the "darkie" drivers were said to have been "pompous-swelled."[4] Negroes picking banjos and singing old plantation melodies provided evening music. The young gentlemen sang Spanish love songs or popular airs to their ladyloves.

South of Amelia Island lay Fort George Island, a longtime summer resort for inland Floridians. Its picturesque vistas and healthful climate began attracting wealthy Northerners in the 1870s and 1880s. However, the popularity of the island was destined to be short-lived.

In the early days travelers visiting the island by boat came ashore at the little village of Pilot Town. The main island, separated by a salt creek, was reached by crossing a rustic bridge. Visitors found the scenery enchanting—the sea to the right, and to the left, large shell mounds draped with lush vegetation rising above the salt meadows. Many visitors felt the scenery united the northern and southern zones with both the more northern trees and the semi-tropical palms.

The island's history was marked by clashes between the Spanish, French, and Indians. The Spanish Governor of St. Augustine first made a grant of the island

Palmetto Avenue, Fort George Island, c. 1869.

A majestic avenue of palms leading to the old plantation called Homestead, for a century the home of the slave-lords of the island.

Booklet, Fort George Island Company, 1887.

Ruins of the old slave cabins, Fort George Island, c. 1900.

Almost a century before, some six hundred slaves were kept on the old Kingsley plantation. Captain Kingsley, often called the king of Fort George, married an African princess and left his estate to his mulatto descendants.

to a man named McQueen, who in turn sold it to a man who lost it on a mortgage foreclosure to a Scotsman named Captain Kingsley. Kingsley, a shrewd despot, ruled for many years as a planter, slaver, and buccaneer.

In 1868, the island was bought by a man from New Hampshire, who began selling small tracts of land for winter residences. A hotel was built close to the ocean and nearby, on a ninety-foot hill, was an observatory. Beyond lay Point Isabel, a lovely feature of the island. Under the shade of moss-draped oaks was a rustic seat where one could gaze at the rolling surf and the white beaches of nearby Talbot Island.

In 1887, the Fort George Island Company, made up of wealthy Northerners, including the venerable General Sherman and Harriet Beecher Stowe, issued an elaborate brochure which promoted a magnificent hotel, one thousand cottage and villa sites, twenty-seven miles of avenues, and the finest shell drives in Florida. One section, Magnolia Park, with about fifty acres of home sites, had the highest elevation on the coast south of the New Jersey Highlands.

Other boat landings were built, one on the Fort George Inlet near the new Fort George Hotel and the other along the St. Johns River near the Beach House (built in 1883). The landings were thronged when the mail arrived with colorful equipages—double carriages, phaetons with fringed tops, high yellow dogcarts—all with fast horses or fine mules, a fashionable turnout for the winter colony residents.

The dream ended abruptly in 1887 when an epidemic of yellow fever discouraged winter visitors. The Fort George Hotel burned in 1888, while unoccupied, and the popular Beach House was dismantled in 1889. The disastrous winter freeze of 1895 ruined the beautiful groves and many tropical trees of great value. The island's golden moment was gone. ▪

From Fernandina tourists could take a day's journey by rail to the Gulf coast and the quaint little village of Cedar Keys, a community chiefly engaged in lumbering and seafaring activities.[1] From Cedar Keys, the traveler could take a steamer to various points along the Gulf.

Outside Fernandina, the traveler saw forests of pine, live oaks, and salt marshes; inland, miles of low pine lands made a monotonous landscape. At Baldwin, passengers could change trains for Talla-hassee, Jacksonville, and other north Florida stops. During the Civil War the town received big headlines ("Baldwin Is Ours") in the New York *Herald*. However, a New England reporter, after his train had jumped the track, stated that its importance was overrated. Baldwin had only four or five buildings in 1875, with two used as hotels. The reporter and his party chose the Farmer's Hotel, adver-tised as having a hunter in the Gulf Hum-mocks to provide delicacies for the table,

View of the sink or disap-pearing lake at Gainesville, c. 1902.

"About a mile from the city is a great natural curiosity called the "sink." Some years ago this was dry land, producing large crops of cane. Subsequently, during a protracted rain storm, this sink or prairie began to fill with water, until a tract sev-eral miles in extent was entirely submerged and has so remained. It is now the recipient of several streams, and has a subterra-nean passage to the sea." (From a diary, 1875.)

Council Oak, Micanopy, c. 1875. Photograph by Furlong & Engle.

During the Seminole Indian Wars, Micanopy was a military post. If a traveler wished to visit the historic area, he could take a mail stage from Gainesville which ran three times a week in 1869.

along with famed Cedar Keys oysters. They found both nonexistent, but the poor food was of no consequence as compared to a restless night combating "full-grown mosquitos" and a choir composed of millions of frogs who "entertained us with a glorious rehearsal."

The next interesting station, Gainesville, was a town reminiscent of western frontier settlements with sandy, littered streets and little shade. Law and order were said to have been remiss here, as they were in so many early Florida settlements. One story told to newcomers was about an itinerant photographer who shot a billiard saloon keeper in an argument over cigars. The photographer was thought to have escaped to Texas but was sighted in town once after the shooting. Nevertheless, Gainesville was regarded as a healthful resort for invalids, and many doctors praised the area above all others.

After leaving Gainesville, the train passed hilly limestone country with open forests and beyond, in lower areas, was an occasional stand of cypress and hummock. Travelers described the train as primitive, recounting a history of jerks and jolts. Some passengers were reported to have been injured in falls from the flat cars. As the Gulf neared, those aboard the swaying train were dubious about the fragile looking trestle which stretched across the islands from the mainland to the Gulf terminus at Cedar Keys. Built

The lighthouse, Sea Horse Key, entrance to Cedar Keys Harbor, 1871.
"The harbor is very shoal, but narrow winding channels lead to the town on Way Key.... The village is prettily situated on a mound which is shaded completely by grand old live-oaks. Long moss hangs in wondrous profusion from the limbs." (Lithograph from *Harper's New Monthly Magazine*, 1871.)

upon two keys connected by a small ferry boat, the town with its coquina-stone buildings and shell streets resembled an old Spanish seaport and was a supply depot for sportsmen.

If money were no object, a sportsman could secure a boat with sailing master at four to five dollars a day—"but I may remark that many of the boatmen along the coast have acquired a weakness, and if peace is desired the whiskey bottle must be kept under lock and key."

Hotel accommodations were primitive even at $2.50 to $3.50 a day. Lodgings improved by 1885 with five hotels, and a restaurant kept by a Swiss gentleman provided Roquefort cheese, good French wine, and other delicacies. Visitors enjoyed the local oysters, which were easily obtained along the bay, and the custom of roasting them shared much the same tradition with the clambakes along the Atlantic coast resorts.

One tourist of 1891 recalled boats that glided from house to house as they did in Venice, and that only one street was not navigable: "The panorama of alternate land and water, with gay gondolas and residences is very fascinating."[2]

Many tourists, who wished to tour the northwest part of the state, boarded a steamer for Pensacola, the site of early Spanish and English settlements. The scene as the traveler neared Pensacola Bay was unforgettable, with long stretches of sandy beach and luxuriant forest converging to the distant harbor. As the vessel steamed closer to shore, the tall lighthouse, with a background of dark green trees and white cottages against the inviting beaches, made a lovely vista. The visitor passed the ruins of Fort McRee, opposite Fort Pickens, the latter standing straight and sturdy at the end of historic

Driving a pair of prize gray mules in an unidentified north Florida town, c. 1900.

Santa Rosa Island with its mighty guns looking out to sea. In the distance stood the remains of old Fort Barrancas, rich with memories of General Jackson and the Spanish commandant who blew it up when the American army captured the place in 1812.

About a mile east of Fort Barrancas, on the mainland, the large buildings of the navy yard loomed on the horizon, "the great derricks holding aloft boilers for expectant hulls."[3] The lower part of Pensacola had a nautical atmosphere with sandy streets crowded with motley groups of mariners busily talking about life at sea, ships, and cargoes. One tourist wondered about a "strangely out of place...back country ox-cart whose great broad wooden-tired wheels and crates of "gonies" or land-turtles rolls silently over sand."[4]

View of Pensacola Harbor, c. 1900.

Fort Barrancas, c. 1900.

A more formidable fortress than the earlier San Carlos, Fort Barrancas was situated just west of the Navy Yard and below was the Pensacola Lighthouse. The two made a pleasant and interesting excursion for the tourist.

The huge wharves, edged with forests of spars and masts, were picturesque with small iron steamers beside great three-masted vessels, all ready to share in the shipping of large quantities of lumber which later in the century were brought to the docks by the train load.

Palafox Street, Pensacola, c. 1884. Photograph by John A. Walker.

Palafox was the principal street of the town. In 1869 there were no accommodations except boarding houses. By 1886, the town had six hotels, averaging from two to four dollars per day.

Variety store, Pensacola, c. 1884. Photograph by John A. Walker.

On the steps of the Leon Hotel, Tallahassee, c. 1886. Photograph by Alvin S. Harper.

An announcement in the *St. Augustine News*, on January 18, 1891, said that the Leon Hotel (Florida's Parlor Hotel) opened its season on New Year's Day with a fine orchestra playing in the afternoon and evening. Other entertainments were weekly hops, beautiful drives, and fine boating and fishing on nearby lakes. Also the hotel offered tennis courts, Eastern cooks, Western meats, and excellent Jersey milk and cream. Best of all, it had rooms with baths!

If the tourist wished to visit Tallahassee, the easiest way was to take a steamer to St. Marks on the Gulf and connect there with a short railroad line to the state capital. Train connections were uncertain, running about once a week when a steamer was in port.

When Sidney Lanier, Southern poet and author, visited Tallahassee in 1875, he took a carriage from the depot and soon found himself opposite the capitol building in front of a "genuine old-fashioned tavern, with a long double piazza running along the entire front…[met by] a neat colored 'Auntie' who took charge of our bags and ushered us into our quarters."[5] Lanier not only liked the hilly coun-

The Kentucky Club at Meridian plantation, c. 1885. Photograph by Alvin S. Harper, Tallahassee.

Washington Square, Tallahassee, c. 1882. Photograph by Kilburn Brothers.

Washington Square, where visitors left their vehicles while shopping or visiting in town, was always a hub of activity.

tryside but found the social life and hospitality to be splendid.

According to a Northern visitor back in 1852, the residents of Tallahassee lived handsomely: "The planters generally reside in the city, preferring the social intercourse of the latter to the dull monotony of a plantation life."[6] The war, however, had changed a land of rich plantations, and many had to begin life anew. Despite its reverses, however, the city retained its charm.

A visitor in the early 1890s commented that Tallahassee was compactly built on a hill with the state capitol crowning the top and roads running down the pretty steep sides into the open country all about. Many delightful days could be spent in riding to the various points of interest—estates out of town, a trip to local lakes, or a favorite excursion to the renowned Wakulla Spring, not far from the St. Marks River.

Bicycle Club, Tallahassee, c. 1882. Photograph by Alvin S. Harper.

The standard bicycle (above) had an adjustable step, heavy rubber tires, and a cow horn handlebar. Each bicycle came with a tool bag, a wrench, and an oil can. The cost was about sixty dollars for the largest size (fifty-inch front wheel).

From Tallahassee, the traveler could take the ten-hour journey by rail to Jacksonville. Leaving the city, the train passed some large hillside plantations, still being worked in the 1890s by small groups of Negroes. In the flourishing town of Monticello, a few miles distant, a tourist of 1852 passing through the village on horseback met a New York circus company and also saw an encampment of emigrants from the Carolinas and Georgia on their way to east Florida—a picturesque group resting around fires along the roadside while their animals were feeding nearby. Next the train came to the pretty town of Madison, and soon the traveler reached Ellaville, along the Suwannee River of Stephen Foster fame. The halfway point was Live Oak, a junction where several rail lines crossed. Another twelve miles brought the train to Wellborn, the gateway to the famous Suwannee River and White Sulphur Springs. From there travelers could take a daily stage to White Sulphur Springs, a few miles away. The fare was two dollars in 1869. Hotel accommodations were three dollars daily or forty dollars a month. A physician from Maine resided at the hotel which catered to those suffering from rheumatism and skin diseases. Nearby was Suwannee Springs, a fashionable summer watering place for Floridians, from the 1840s.

The remainder of the tour, with the exception of Lake City, held little interest for the traveler. However, on entering Jacksonville, the visitor to Florida found by the mid-1870s a prosperous city with good hotels and wide, shaded streets, a pleasant homecoming after traveling so many miles and seeing so many diverse attractions. ▪

**On the Suwannee at
Ellaville, c. 1900.**

When Sidney Lanier stepped from the train in Jacksonville in January of 1874, he noticed a pleasant splash among the lily pads underneath the platform, and when he lifted his eyes, he saw the great expanse of the St. Johns River stretching to the south and east, a wondrous sight to a weary traveler.

The railroad depot was but a few yards from the Grand National Hotel. Visitors to the establishment arriving in the evening hours were greeted by strains of music drifting from the windows of the brilliantly lit hotel, and seldom were the streets empty of promenaders from the larger hotels. The winter season was usually ushered in on New Year's Day with grand balls and parties beckoning the cream of society from all over the country and abroad.

Railroad station, National Hotel in background, c. 1874. Photograph by C. Seaver, Jr.

Where Sidney Lanier first stepped from the train in Jacksonville, in January, 1874.

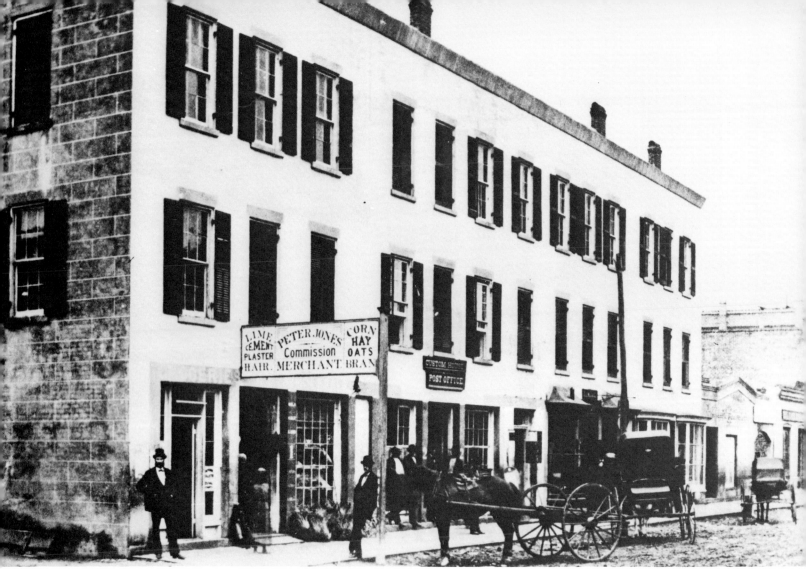

Post Office and Custom House, Bay Street, c. 1872. Photograph by E. & H.T. Anthony.

Crowds gathered here during the winter season to wait for mail from home.

Despite its reputation as a winter resort, Jacksonville did not always escape wintry blasts. During frosty periods of chilly north winds, doors were closed, log fires lit, and extra blankets brought out of hiding. Visitors deserted balconies and drank more whiskey than ice water!

On sunny days curious visitors promenaded along the sidewalks, crowding the post office and visiting the fruit stores. Palmetto-braiders did a brisk business in hats, and curiosity shops were always filled with tourists buying trinkets to take back north. Novelties like sea-beans, made into vest or sleeve buttons, were popular as well as alligators' teeth, plumes

Jacksonville, Fla., _____ 1885.

Mr C H Chase

Bought of **M. MEYERSON,**

—JEWELER,—

And Manufacturer of Florida Curiosities,

No. 24 Hogan Street.

3 Watch Charms	1 50
1 pr Sleve Buttons	1 25
3 Scarf Pins	1 95
4 Bangles	2 00
1 Broach	1 25
1 Compass Charm	50
1 Task Mounted	50
1 Nick Lace	75
1 Bear Tusk Pin	2 50
1 Eye Glass Spring	1 50
Rec Payment	$ 13 70
M Meyerson	

Souvenirs the tourists were buying in 1885.

Live baby alligator, 1896. Photograph by Jesse S. Wooley.

"They put them in cigar boxes alive and the tourist carried them with him along with others that are stuffed and mounted."

of herons and curlews' feathers, cranes'-wings, angel fish, canes made of mangrove or orange-wood, coral branches, and coquina figures. Alligators' teeth were made into whistles, watch chains, and other popular items. One large curiosity dealer in Florida offered from four to six dollars a pound for such teeth, depending on size.

The more serious-minded visitors found the circulating library near the National Hotel on Bay Street a quiet spot to while away a few hours. Every morning a vendor in the library sold current newspapers and magazines. The reading room of Ambler's Bank also welcomed visitors. The more daring and adventuresome on a visit to the wharf, not far from the National Hotel, could secure a pleasant sailboat for hire at seventy-five cents an hour. For the equestrian, livery stables offered saddle-horses and buggies and carriages for riding about town.

One of the favorite drives was to Moncrief's Spring, about four miles from town near a creek of the same name. At the time of Lanier's visit the mineral spring had been taken over by a company which was constructing bathhouses, separate for men and women, each sixty feet long by fifteen feet wide. A restaurant, bowling alley, dance pavilion, and one-mile race course were also being built.

Ticket office, Savannah-Florida Steamers, Bay Street, c. 1871. Photograph by W.H. Cushing.

The landscaping of town residences and the artistically arranged promenades pleased visitors to Jacksonville. Picturesque live-oak trees from which hung graceful strands of gray moss overshadowed sidewalks of plank and brick. By the 1880s many changes had taken place. Northern money and enterprise made Jacksonville a thriving metropolis. Alligators no longer rested but a stone's throw from the Court House. Sportsmen found fewer wild turkeys, deer, and partridge, and even the river provided less fish for the townspeople.

In January and February the glitter of the shops was irrestible to the tourists, and the throngs of people mingling on the streets presented a cosmopolitan scene. Long-haired westerners and Texans, with their eye-catching clothing, walked side by side with the latest "dude" from New York or Boston. Fine ladies in Paris fashions rubbed elbows with laughing Negro women in informal prints. A gentlemen from Kentucky could be seen walking arm in arm with an ex-planter from Virginia, both smoking furiously and loudly talking politics. Providing a native flavor to the scene were a couple of "crackers," noted for their speckled and corpselike faces, hands in pockets, lack-luster eyes, and open mouths.[1]

Florida cracker with cart, corner Forsythe and Ocean streets, c. 1879.

From the National Hotel, Bay Street, c. 1874. Photograph by C. Seaver, Jr.

The principal thoroughfare in the city was Bay Street. Value of lots fronting the business portion of the street was $175 per foot in 1875. During the winter months, the street was thronged with promenaders visiting the many stores and shops—jewelry, drug, and book stores were among the favorite places for loitering. Also, according to newspaper complaints in 1875, it had a great number of gambling dens, thieves, and bunko artists.

Bicycling, c. 1882.

Jacksonville, with its flat streets, was an ideal place for the bicycling fad in the 1880s and bikes came in many sizes. For short legs, small wheels, and for long legs, large wheels—a size for everyone. The length inside the leg, ran from a standard twenty-eight inches to fifty inches.

The streets also saw a generous sprinkling of Britishers. Young English emigrants were often targets for local "bunko" men, but an English observer said that they were not as easy victims as country boys from Indiana or Ohio, who came to Florida with dollars to buy an orange grove. The well-to-do Englishman was also represented, perhaps as a director of a Florida land company hoping to add to his English income. The rich Englishman was always conspicuous on his horse, especially when he forced a trot, and his female companions were graceful horsewomen pleasant to watch.[2]

Hotel life in Jacksonville in the 1880s was luxurious and costly, but such accommodations made the city a mecca for tourists. The St. James, a magnificent building, formed one whole side of a square and was planted with orange and other decorative trees. The Carleton House, the Everett (the old National), and others followed the same general pattern for opulence. Electric lights illuminated

Boating on the St. Johns, c. 1874. Photograph by C. Seaver, Jr.

Many visitors rented boats at the wharf just a short walk from the hotels for a pleasant outing on the river.

St. James Hotel, c. 1875.

Built in 1869, the St. James featured a bowling alley and billiard rooms. Other additions to the building were made in 1872 and again in 1881. A fire destroyed the hotel in 1901. Rates per day in 1886 were four dollars.

Oliver W., Jr., the racing ostrich, c. 1902.

Exhibitions were given at the ostrich farm, beginning at 11 A.M. and 3:30 P.M. daily.

Advertisement. From *Florida Rambler*, 1873-1875.

The advertisement failed to mention that "The notorious John Morrisey has a club house near the St. James hotel, to which men of means who desire to invest money at a sacrifice, are cordially welcome."

the hotels after sunset, superb dining was provided for guests, and a band usually furnished music for dancing or listening—all made appropriate dwelling places for the Jay Goulds, the Carnegies, and other millionaires. Smaller hotels and boarding houses offered less pretentious quarters for those of modest means.

A typical day might include an elaborate breakfast, reading the Jacksonville *Times*, followed by an hour relaxing on the hotel verandah. A stroll through the city and its markets was often on the daily program with perhaps a telegram being sent along the way. Eating oranges during the day was a ritual as was friendly conversation on the verandah with other guests until supper was announced. The ladies commanded attention after dinner, insisting on music and perhaps dancing before bed.

Florida on wheels, 1895.

The second *Florida's Rolling Exposition* was built in 1887, entirely of native Florida woods, and was valued at $50,000. The outside of the railroad car was finished in buff color to harmonize with carmine and green. Oil paintings lined both sides of the car, displaying selected scenery of Florida's ocean, lakes, and rivers. Decorations of oranges, pineapples, and cocoanuts enhanced the scenic works of art. Also, inside the car were displays of just about everything Florida produced.

From 1876, one of the winter tourist attractions was the Florida Exposition and State Fair. In February, 1880, it included a Grand Military Review of Artillery and Infantry Corps, a fireman's parade, and a magnificent speed ring with entries of celebrated trotting and running horses. Both steamer and railroad companies gave visitors special excursion rates. The 1880 Exposition featured the Ponce de Leon band, paintings by favorite American artists—Bierstadt, Hart, Brown, De Haas, and Moran, a meteor weighing two hundred pounds, a pen full of alligators, a camp of Seminole Indians, flowers, and fruit. One interesting feature was a model Japanese village complete with streets. By 1890, the Exposition was usually open from early January until about the first of April.

The attraction of Jacksonville to the winter tourist lasted into the 1890s, and as one 1892 visitor said, the city might have been mistaken for Long Branch (New Jersey's famous resort) in July: "With its great hotels illuminated from top to basements, its sounds of dance music in all the great parlors, and the array of long porches crowded with ease-taking men and women in flannels and

View of Jacksonville, c. 1877.

The steady growth and prosperity of the town reflected its growing lumber industry and tourist trade. The city in 1875 was lighted with gas, had a fire department, a National bank, a Freedman's bank, and two private banks.

Twelve churches were ample to supply the demand for all religious sects. The better class of house, built in 1875, was two stories with double verandas—with seven or eight rooms, built substantially, the cost was from $1,200 to $2,000.

Florida Sub-tropical Exposition, 1891.

"It is opening day of Florida's Sub-tropical Exposition. Verdant arches cross the city's broad streets, and these arches are gold-starred with real oranges in wanton profusion. Stone facades are a mass of decoration. Many homes have been turned into fern-covered bowers. In the afternoon the exposition was formally opened with a grand parade—a moving parade of the trades of the city of Jacksonville, rich in devices and symbolic tributes to the genius of commerce. Then came the formal ceremonies at the Exposition Building."

tennis caps and russet slippers and gossamer gowns.... There were the same laughter and chatter and rollicking semi-grown children; the same aimless but happy couples keeping slow measured tread on the pavements; the frames of staring photographs, the nickel in the slot machines, the shops full of gimcrack souvenirs made in Germany and New York, the peanuts and soda-water, the odor of perfumery, the rustle of silks, the peeping slippers—the very same; all the same."[3]

Display counter, State Fair, 1876.

The first State Fair was held in Jacksonville, in March of 1876. It featured, besides all the wonderful flowers, the famous Florida orange in all of its many shapes, sizes, and flavors, and a gigantic 15½-inch lemon (through the center); shells, sea-beans, rattlesnake skins and, thanks to the ladies of Jacksonville, an elaborate display of their handiwork.

The Yacht Club, c. 1900.
"Among the beaches of the water front is the yacht clubhouse, a beautiful building on piers with locks and reservoirs for boats and sculls, and a handsome assembly room above; perhaps the most delightful resort for youthful recreation on the Atlantic Coast." (From the *South Florida Railroad* brochure of 1886.)

The steamer *Chesapeake* ready for a day's excursion on the St. Johns River, c. 1881. Photograph by J.S. Mitchell.

The invalid population, so prevalent a few years before, had dwindled. By now most of them spent the winters in the piney woods and mountain resorts of Georgia and the Carolinas. Also, the wealthy tourists turned to St. Augustine after Henry Flagler built his palatial hotels in the late 1880s, and by 1896 Jacksonville's prestigious years as a tourist resort came to an end when the railroad brought the wealthy tourists to a new tropical paradise—the Palm Beaches and Miami. ■

A trip by riverboat steamer along the wild and weird St. Johns River was perhaps the greatest attraction for all Florida tourists. While gliding along the grand course of the river, the visitor saw along the banks flourishing little towns, villages, and large estates, luxuriant orange groves, and exotic tropical vegetation: "Herons and cranes watch saucily from the riverbank, and monster turtles and still more montrous alligators slide slowly along, only to duck their heads at the flash of the gun or pistol." It was a panorama completely different to Northern eyes, one remembered vividly long after the excursion was over.

The St. Johns River, unique in its northward flow of four hundred miles, turned abruptly eastward in the vicinity of Jacksonville and emptied into the Atlantic Ocean. Large steamers from New York, Savannah, and Charleston made regular runs south from Jacksonville to Palatka,

The *City of Jacksonville*, near departure time, on the afternoon of February 2, 1896. Photograph by Jesse S. Wooley.

"A very pleasant journey which no Florida tourist should miss is that up the St. Johns River by boat from Jacksonville to Sanford. The steamer *City of Jacksonville* and her captain, William A. Shaw, are among the very best of their kinds, and whosoever accompanies them will find by the time the pretty part of the river is reached, above Palatka, the passengers will have been brought together into something like a family circle, on good terms with one another."

ST. JOHNS RIVER SERVICE.

JACKSONVILLE TO SANFORD, FLA.,

...AND...

INTERMEDIATE LANDINGS.

STEAMERS:

"CITY OF JACKSONVILLE"

...AND...

"FREDERICK DeBARY."

DIRECT CONNECTIONS FROM BOSTON and all EASTERN POINTS.

Take this Line and avoid passage along rough New England Coast.

CLOSE CONNECTIONS made at Charleston, S.C., with South Carolina & Georgia R.R., for Augusta, Columbia, Macon, Atlanta, and all interior points. At Jacksonville, Fla., with St. Johns River Service, Florida Central & Peninsular R.R., Florida East Coast Railway, and Jacksonville, Tampa & Key West Railway for all points in Florida.

☞ ALL SHIPS TOUCH AT CHARLESTON, AFFORDING AMPLE OPPORTUNITY TO VIEW THE CITY.

For Sailing Schedules, Plans of Steamers and further information, call on or address

or the undersigned,

J. A. FLANDERS, Eastern Agent, 201 Washington Street, BOSTON,

M. H. CLYDE, Ass't Traffic Manager. A. J. COLE, Gen'l Passenger Agent. THEO. G. EGER, Traffic Manager.

WM. P. CLYDE & CO., General Agents, 5 Bowling Green, NEW YORK.

R. A. SUPPLY CO., BOSTON.

Clyde Line brochure, 1896.

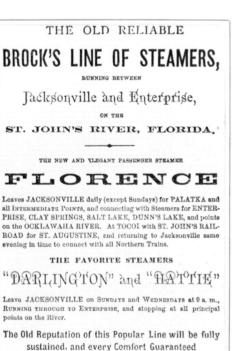

THE OLD RELIABLE

BROCK'S LINE OF STEAMERS,

RUNNING BETWEEN

Jacksonville and Enterprise,

ON THE

ST. JOHN'S RIVER, FLORIDA.

THE NEW AND ELEGANT PASSENGER STEAMER

FLORENCE

Leaves JACKSONVILLE daily (except Sundays) for PALATKA and all INTERMEDIATE POINTS, and connecting with Steamers for ENTERPRISE, CLAY SPRINGS, SALT LAKE, DUNN'S LAKE, and points on the OCKLAWAHA RIVER. At TOCOI with ST. JOHN'S RAILROAD for ST. AUGUSTINE, and returning to Jacksonville same evening in time to connect with all Northern Trains.

THE FAVORITE STEAMERS

"DARLINGTON" and "HATTIE"

Leave JACKSONVILLE on SUNDAYS and WEDNESDAYS at 9 a. m., RUNNING THROUGH to Enterprise, and stopping at all principal points on the River.

The Old Reputation of this Popular Line will be fully sustained, and every Comfort Guaranteed to its Patrons.

JACOB BROCK, Agent,

Jacksonville, Fla.

Advertisement. *Florida Rambler***, 1873-1875.**

and from there, because of shallow water, passengers transferred to smaller steamers which plied onward to Lake Monroe and Enterprise. Also, from Palatka, steamers could bring travelers for a trip along the Ocklawaha River to Silver Springs or into the interior lake regions.

Local steamers left Jacksonville, usually a good two hours late, at eleven in the morning. However, time passed quickly for a traveler watching the bustling activity at the wharf—the drays driven by Negroes bringing all kinds of merchandise, household goods, lumber, chickens, fertilizers, and a multitude of other things, including mail for delivery at the innumerable landings along the river.

Typical of local steamers running from Jacksonville to Enterprise—a 206-mile trip—was the *Darlington*, a boat referred to in many travel accounts. The fare in 1869 was nine dollars, including meals and stateroom, for the thirty-six-hour trip. Built similar to a western riverboat, it carried about forty passengers, with the first deck given over to machinery and freight and the upper deck to passengers. Two "saloons" were featured—a small one for women and children, and the main saloon, surrounded by staterooms, which also served as a dining hall.

Captain Jacob Brock was the master and owner of the vessel and also the proprietor of the well-known Brock Hotel at the end of the line in Enterprise. Admiral Rose, a legendary figure in the folklore of the region, ruled supreme. Her sharp commands were heard above the din and confusion at every landing. A woman of stout build and piercing eyes, she spoke the final word in her every tone and gesture.[1]

Many tourists did not take the entire journey to Enterprise, but made brief excursions or stopovers along the way. Each landing brought all passengers on deck to see the new arrivals or departures. It was here that local merchants could hawk their wares or homesteaders

A tourist recounted: "From the lofty decks of the steamers a great deal is seen, but every moment one is hurried ruthlessly away from some spot where there is every temptation to linger, and then left to while away hours at some landing where preceding crowds have gathered every flower, and alarmed every bird with pistols and parasols."

could receive long-awaited items or welcome letters from home.

As the steamer wended its way southward, the first settlement of interest was Orange Park, a picturesque village with a fine winter hotel, a river road fringed by handsome live oaks, an attractive wharf house, and a long pier. Next came the small settlement of Mandarin, distinguished by the winter residence of Harriet Beecher Stowe. The cottage was situated on a twelve-foot bluff, just a few rods from the landing pier. Travelers always hoped to catch a glimpse of the Stowe family, and hundreds of visitors stopped by to see the author of *Uncle Tom's Cabin*.

The next stop after Mandarin was Hibernia, a resort which featured a boarding house with a delightful promenade —a river walk about three-quarters of a mile long, overhung with graceful live oaks. Boats could be obtained, and boarders found pleasant recreation in picnics and fishing expeditions. Rooms were fifteen dollars a week.

Three miles past Hibernia, the steamer put in at Magnolia, an old resort built in 1851 by Dr. W. D. Benedict; in 1869, two doctors from Massachusetts enlarged the buildings, made repairs, and refurbished the hotel to accommodate one hundred guests with respiratory problems. By the 1890s, Magnolia became a fashionable hotel resort, one catering to a completely different clientele. The famous Clyde steamers made daily stops at the Magnolia Springs Hotel, a modern building with an elevator, baths, electric bells and lights, many rooms with fireplaces, and a swimming pool. The management offered special inducements to its guests—a darkroom for amateur photographers, tennis courts, and hunting dogs and guides for sportsmen. Rowboats and a steam launch

Casa Nova Hotel, Orange Park, from the wharf, 1892.

Traveling south from Jacksonville, the Casa Nova was the first of many large and comfortable hotels along the St. Johns River.

Harriet Beecher Stowe's home, Mandarin, c. 1873. Photograph attributed to C. Seaver, Jr.

The famous author of *Uncle Tom's Cabin* seated on the porch with her husband the professor, and her daughters.

Schoolhouse and church, Mandarin, c. 1878. Photograph by C. Seaver, Jr.

Sylvia Sunshine (Amanda Brook, of Tennessee) wrote about a Sunday church service in 1879: "Mrs. Harriet Beecher Stowe is here today.... The service was opened by a very long prayer from Dr. Stowe after which he preached a purely orthodox sermon on the subject of godliness. Mrs. Harriet had confidence in the ability of her husband ... and went to sleep.

for picnic excursions were available. The third annual U.S. National Tennis tournament was held at the hotel in 1893, and guests came from all over the country. The event, which lasted several days, featured among its entertainments a cake walk, a grand march, and a piano recital.

Only two miles from Magnolia was one of the most popular resorts along the river, Green Cove Springs. The town's main attraction was a remarkably clear mineral spring emitting three thousand gallons of water per minute. Its temperature of seventy-five degrees made it ideal for bathing. An 1874 visitor, in describing the famous Blue Sulphur Spring, said that bubbles came up from a ravine and flowed through buildings used

Advertisement. From the
Hotel Red Book Directory, **1886.**

Magnolia Springs Hotel, 1891. Photograph by O. Pierre Havens.

A leisurely life for the fashionable clientele. Wharf and summerhouse in background.

Gail Borden's Park, Green Cove Springs, 1892.

"About two years ago Honorable John G. Borden, the great condensed milk manufacturer, purchased a 400-acre tract, which he is laying out in parks, courts, drives, circles and avenues. A valuable addition." (From *Jacksonville, Florida and Surrounding Towns*, 1889-90.)

for bathing. After paying an admission of twenty-five cents, the patron entered a twenty-five-by-sixty-foot area enclosed by a high board fence. Small dressing rooms were on a platform from which visitors descended into a bath of clear blue water, which showed white sand at a depth of about four feet. Regular bathing hours were assigned separately for men and women.

One party visiting Green Cove Springs was greeted at the dock by two black fellows shouting the praises of the Clarendon Hotel and the Palmetto House. Luggage from the steamer was brought to the Clarendon located next to the bathing enclosure. However, all members of the party could not be accommodated at the hotel, and some stayed at the nearby Palmetto House, an old hostelry standing on the edge of a palmetto jungle. A low roof enclosed the piazzas on both sides, contributing to its venerable charm.

A novel feature of each hotel was the outdoor lighting. On the top of four-foot posts were brick-covered shallow boxes, about three feet square. Pine knots were lighted from beneath the boxes and flames burned brightly during the evening hours, silhouetting the village against the somber forest background, giving the whole an aura of mystery for romantic nineteenth-century visitors. Guests were entertained watching the youth of the village dance in the firelight, a cheerful note in a shadowy setting.

Spring Bath Houses, Clarendon Hotel in background, Green Cove Springs, c. 1874. Photograph by C. Seaver, Jr.

"The Springs, with the Clarendon Hotel adjoining, are but a short distance from the river-bank. Connected with this hotel are hot and cold baths, and swimming baths, of springwaters. These waters…have a temperature of 76°F." (Sidney Lanier, 1876).

Residence of William King, Mandarin, March, 1878. Photograph by C. Seaver, Jr.

William King, from New Jersey, typifies the enterprising Northerner who came to Florida during the 1870s and 1880s. Arriving in 1873, he cleared the land, built a prestigious home, and planted 175 orange trees. In March of 1878, he built a steamboat wharf and waiting room for the convenience of the townspeople.

Clarendon House,

GREEN COVE SPRINGS, Fla.

ON THE

ST. JOHN'S RIVER,

30 Miles South of Jacksonville.

Daily Mail and two daily Steamers from Jacksonville to Green Cove.

Belonging to this house, and within 100 ft. of it, is the Green Cove Warm Sulphur Spring, discharging 3,000 gallons per minute, of temperature 78°.

This water is highly valuable in its medicinal qualities, in the following diseases. Rheumatism—Gout—Scrofula—Dyspepsia—Paralysis—Neuralgia—all Nervous Affections—Erysipelas, and all Eruptive Diseases—Kidney Disorders, and General Debility.

Large additions have been made, during the past season, to the Bathing facilities. The Baths and Dressing Rooms now occupy a space 200 ft. long by 50 ft. wide.

The house is supplied with water from the Spring, by means of water power.

HARRIS, APPLEGATE & CO., Proprietors.

The Florida Express, Clarendon House, Green Cove Springs, c. 1874. Photograph by C. Seaver, Jr.

A family keepsake photograph to fit the stereo-viewer back home.

Gents Bathing Pool, Green Cove Springs, April 3, 1883.

By the early 1880s, a new generation of bathers had taken over, and the crude swimming hole and rickety bathhouses of 1870 were but a dim memory.

Gents Bathing Pool   Green Cove Springs Fla.

The Tocoi Landing, c. 1874. Photograph by E. & H.T. Anthony.

Charles Hallock wrote of his experiences along the St. Johns in a handbook for sportsmen: "At Tocoi we found the *Hattie* awaiting us—a small steamer, but necessarily so, as the rest of our trip was to be made in narrow streams and shoal water. We were very comfortable on board of her. The table was good, quarters clean and the captain— Charlie Brock—a good fellow."

Wedding Day, Palatka, April 4, 1876. Photograph by W.H. Cushing.

Everyone came to the wedding including the bride's pet, a great blue heron.

About fourteen miles from Green Cove Springs, visitors reached the site of an ancient Spanish settlement, although no vestige of interest remained. It was here at the Picolata landing that St. Augustine passengers disembarked. One 1870 visitor told of the dreadful conditions: "A shaky wooden pier at which steamers discharge their burdens; a one-story shanty, and a ten-foot square grog-shop on the shore."[2] Soon after, steamers began stopping at the Tocoi landing, about two miles farther south.

On leaving Tocoi, the St. Johns widened and narrowed before reaching Palatka, the most important town along the river. According to Lanier, the citizens of the town were divided as to whether the spelling should be Pilatka or Palatka (photographs, maps, and guide books often used Pilatka).

One interesting sidelight of pioneer days in Palatka was recounted by an early tourist on January 9, 1843: "Genl. Worth, Wife, & two Daughters started for Tampa Bay & Mrs. Van Buren for Cedar Keys to meet her husband—Mrs. V. B. is a daughter of Doct. Mott of New York married some two months ago—The young ladies were mounted on fine horses & looked quite *formidable* with their black riding dresses, a side sash for belts, & thin long dirks—They had an escort of 12 soldiers, together with 10 ambulances each having its driver & 5 mules which formed quite a caravan."[3]

By the 1850s many men of wealth had settled in the town and on nearby planta-

tions. The village resembled New England with its handsome residences on tree-lined streets, and two excellent boarding houses had been built for tourists. After the Civil War more Northern settlers migrated to the settlement, and they found anti-Yankee sentiment to be very strong among the local crackers and backwoodsmen. Sometimes parties of rough horsemen rode into town with bowie knives, and shooting affrays and bloody fights were not uncommon.

By 1870 Palatka was a thriving village with several stores, including a drug store, two churches, two steam mills, and two saw mills. Two large hotels had opened, the Putnam House and the St. Johns House. Both charged $3.50 a day. The latter was said to have been blessed with wholesome, well-cooked food. Palatka continued as a tourist town, especially with the coming of the railroads. By the mid-1880s it was on the main line of the Jacksonville, Tampa, and Key West Railroad.

The first Putnam House, April 14, 1881 (destroyed by fire, 1884).

The new Putnam House, 1891.

Palatka's most prestigious hotel rose from the ashes of the great 1884 conflagration. The owner, Oscar Barron, continued welcoming guests to the establishment with no increase in rates—$2.50 to $3.00 per day.

St. Johns Hotel, c. 1873. Photograph by Rufus Morgan.

One of Palatka's new small hotels in the 1870s. A few years later Mr. Peterman, the owner, sold out and opened a saloon.

Advertisement. *Florida Rambler*, 1873-1875.

J.P Miller's band, Palatka, c. 1873. Photograph by W.H. Cushing.

The visiting band, from Norwich, Connecticut, must have caused a sensation among the townspeople and winter tourists. It was undoubtedly the biggest and best band south of Jacksonville.

Short-stay visitors in Palatka could take steamers to favorite tourist attractions—Dunn's Lake or Silver Springs. Passengers going to Enterprise by the steamers *Florence, Darlington,* or *Hattie* made overnight stops at Palatka, giving travelers a few hours to look over the town.

Outside Palatka, the river narrowed, the vegetaion became more tropical, and many travelers recalled March as the month when flowers along the bank were in perfection and, on a moonlit night, enchanting—the lilies, palms, and cypresses formed unforgettable pictures as the steamer wended its way along the crooked stream.

Lemon Street, Palatka, c. 1873. Photograph by W.H. Cushing.

The office space above the store building was occupied by a dentist and an attorney. A news item about the disastrous fire of November 7, 1884, noted: "That Mr. B.L. Lilienthal's furniture store was not burned is almost a miracle, and it was the only building left standing on the block. As it was it looked several times as if it would surely go."

Heiss's Old Curiosity Shop interior, Palatka, c. 1875. Photograph by Irving Haas.

This shop was where visitors to Palatka could find something of interest: "He has a tank containing a large number of living alligators, ranging in size from the infant specimens to one eight foot long. He also shows tame coons, live otters, squirrels and several specimens of birds. His museum of stuffed specimens is quite extensive. Here is the 'Centennial alligator,' 15 feet long, and monster rattlesnakes and moccasins."

Heiss's Old Curiosity Shop. "Where Georgia bought her alligator, Feb. 12, 1875." Photograph by J.F. Mears.

Waterfront, Palatka, 1892.

A Jacksonville steamer arriving at dock, and a Silver Springs excursion boat about to leave.

About twenty miles south, the steamer reached Welaka, an old-time resort and the site of an old Indian village and early Spanish settlement. The town, opposite the mouth of the Ocklawaha River, had a fine hotel near some excellent sulphur springs.

Beyond Welaka, the St. Johns widened into Little Lake George and then into Lake George proper, a beautiful expanse of water about eighteen miles long and twelve miles wide. Flocks of herons, white curlews, cranes, pelicans, and other varieties of birds made the lake their home and provided a delightful retreat for naturalists. At the southern end of the lake was the sizeable Drayton Island, noted for fruit growing and its remarkable Indian mounds.

Eggleston's Florida Shell Store, and Eggleston and Miller, Taxidermists, Palatka, c. 1879.

"Where a very large alligator is about to be skinned."

The Silver Springs steamer *Ocklawaha* docked at the ice house, Palatka, c. 1873. Photograph by E. & H.T. Anthony.

J.C. Canova, from Cuba, owned the first ice house, and for a number of years the only one in Florida.

The steamer *Chattahoochee* heading for Jacksonville glides past Jessie Dakin. Off Racimo, 1888. Photograph by Leonard Dakin.

Front porch, Dakin residence, Racimo (near Georgetown), March 24, 1888.

Photographed by Leonard Dakin, amateur photographer, about whom Edward Steichen wrote: "contributes a unique document to the Americana of his time." Dakin's future wife, Jessie, is seated on right.

A family trip (goodbyes). The Dakin wharf, Racimo, March 6, 1891. Photograph by Leonard Dakin.

Afternoon tea, linen, and china. George W.B. Dakin, wife Anne Maria, and daughter Florence, Racimo, 1887. Photograph by Leonard Dakin.

Jessie Dakin, pole fishing, Georgetown, 1888. Photograph by Leonard Dakin.

Passengers could stop at Seville Landing, about halfway up Lake George, and by telegraphing ahead could have a carriage waiting for the four-mile trip into town. Oranges were shipped from Seville's many luxuriant groves after the railroad came in 1885.

After passing the many landings, the boat reached the famous Volusia Bar, the site of endless delays and annoyances. Sometimes the water level was as low as three and a half feet so that only the shallowest draught boats could cross. The government removed the obstruction in the early 1880s.

Fives miles beyond the bar was the Volusia landing, an important supply depot for settlers, and soon, on the opposite shore, Astor appeared, with its impressive warehouse and wharf. The town was also the river terminus for the narrow gauge St. Johns and Lake Eustis Railroad, which opened up the lake regions around Eustis and Tavares.

Mr. & Mrs. William K. Lente and hired hand in the garden. The Lente Farm "Nirvana," Seville, c. 1888.

Lente, originally from New York and a longtime winter resident of Palatka, was the organizer and president of the Seville Company and the first postmaster of the new town when the *Florida Times-Union* wrote about it in January of 1886: "The company owns three miles of lake-front lots. Sidewalks have been laid out throughout the business section. Waterworks and a sewage system are being completed. The town has two hotels, several stores, three churches, and a number of residences. Buyers of town lots are required to lay sidewalks and plant shade trees. Sale of liquor is under control."

Vicinity of Astor, St. Johns River, February, 1896.

Orange Grove, Seville, c. 1890. Photograph by William H. Jackson.

William Henry Jackson, the famous photographer of the West, captured here the beauty and very essence of Florida orange-growing with the camera's realistic eye.

Deep River, between Barberville and Spring Garden, c. 1890. Photograph by William H. Jackson.

Bathing Party, De Leon Springs, c. 1890. Photograph by J.A. Enseminger.

The new ice house, DeLand, c. 1885. Photograph by H.S. Cole.

South of Astor, about twelve miles from Lake George, was a colony called Spring Garden, a settlement built near the site of the old Rees plantation where John James Audubon had visited briefly in 1832. In 1872, Major George H. Norris, of New York State, laid out streets, planted orange trees, and built a hotel in the grove, surrounded by a number of small cottages for invalid guests. A nearby landing pier made the settlement self-sufficient. A powerful circular spring, which had operated the sugar mill on the old plantation, was three miles south, and after the railroad reached the area in the mid-1880s the spring, later called De Leon Springs, became a popular place for picnic and bathing parties with its accompanying pavilion and bathhouse, built to entice the tourist trade.

A few miles south was the wharf for DeLand, a village about five miles east of the river. Henry A. DeLand, from Fairport, New York, developed the community, and in 1876 it was named in his honor. Land speculators induced settlers to the town through advertising, and by the 1880s goods and services of all kinds were offered newcomers. Visitors found a charming hotel set in the midst of an orange grove, and a profusion of flowers added to the beauty of the site. A sign reading "Floral Grove," supported by posts with an ornate bird cage on top, suggested hospitality. A garden connected with the hotel provided vegetables and fruits in season—strawberries in January were a treat to Northerners! The owner of a resort hotel in Asbury Park, New Jersey, opened another hotel in December, 1883. Guests, met at the steamboat landing and brought by carriage to the hotel, found a large stable with good horses. Patrons could use carriages for picnic parties to the many local orange groves or newly laid-out subdivisions.

Title page, from *The South*, 1884.

This newspaper, printed by the South Publishing Company, New York, was one of many promotional devices to advise Northern readers about the opportunities offered by the new town of DeLand.

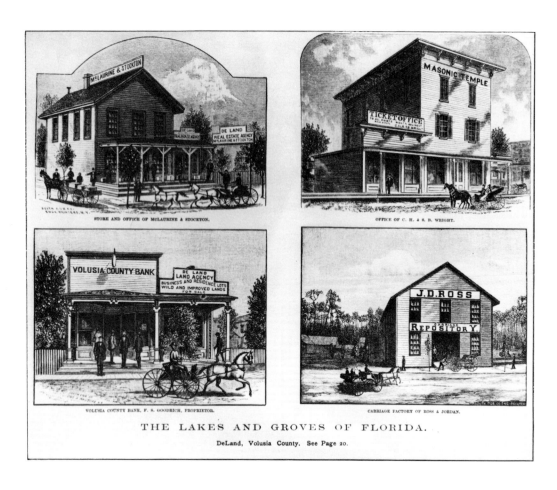

CARRIAGE FACTORY OF ROSS & JORDAN.

THE LAKES AND GROVES OF FLORIDA.

DeLand, Volusia County. See Page 20.

See Page 20.

Real estate promotion, DeLand, 1884.

A multitude of small towns along the St. Johns River were promoted from the 1870s by land agents who not only invested in land, but built small hotels and boarding houses to lure prospective clients. Many of the engravings and lithographs appearing in *The South* were reproduced from photographs taken by Stanley J. Morrow, one of America's most important photographers.

Of the other small settlements passed further south, the most interesting was Blue Springs—a wharf, a road, and a residence on a little hill. The landing was the port for Orange City, two miles inland. Visitors found it difficult to describe the ethereal beauties of the springs—a round pool, about eighty feet in diameter, very deep with an opaque tint to the water: "Its overhanging shade [was] of live oak, palmettos, and vines. A small tent over the stream was the only bathing convenience."[4] The water flowing from the spring enabled steamers to float in so that passengers could look over the side into the crystal water to observe the fish below.

By 1880 a passenger could put ashore at the DeLand or Blue Spring Landing and take a carriage overland to New Smyrna, Daytona, or the Halifax River region.

Newspaper advertisement. From *The South*, 1884.

Later, in 1887, the Atlantic & Western Railroad ran from Blue Springs Landing to New Smyrna.

Continuing southward along the St. Johns, passengers could be transferred at Wekiva to a little craft which would bring them inland to the resorts of Altamonte and Apopka, thriving little settlements with interest in growing oranges and vegetables.

After passing endless marshes and hummocks, the river entered Lake Monroe. Before the 1870s, the settlement of Mellonville (later Sanford) on the south bank of the lake was an important landing for settlers and tourists.

One romantic writer of the 1880s described Sanford: "She sits among her palms, the most distinctly oriental in appearance of South Florida cities. Its typical foliage is redolent of old Arabic tale and mythological fable, and this charm of her picture is infinitely improved by the situation on the broad bosom of Lake Monroe."[5]

On the north bank of the lake, opposite Sanford, was Enterprise. In 1869, passengers may have been somewhat dismayed on viewing the half-dozen buildings. However, they were agreeably surprised by the huge lakeside hotel with attractive green blinds and an airy verandah. Attached to the building was a billiard saloon and ten-pin alley. Room and board was from fifteen to twenty dollars weekly.

A small local steamboat penetrated the marsh to bring sportsmen to the outlying lakes for a pleasant day excursion. It was said that many invalids, after a few weeks of tramping about with gun and fishing rod, became the pictures of health.

Near Enterprise, along the lake, was a large orange grove belonging to Frederick De Bary, a wealthy New Yorker, who came to Enterprise in 1870. He built an imposing residence close to a powerful spring with bathhouses for guests. The spring was also used to force water into a

"Breakfast is Ready." St. Johns River, c. 1878. Photograph by C. Seaver, Jr.

The informality of winter life in Florida was a well-known part of the tourist package. *Decorum*, a book on etiquette and dress for the best American society of 1877, suggested: "The usual costume of gentlemen is white flannel trousers, white rowing jersey, and a straw hat. Pea-jackets are worn when their owners are not absolutely employed in rowing."

The *City of Jacksonville*,
docking at Sanford wharf,
February 3, 1896. Photo-
graph by Jesse S. Wooley.

Advertisement. From the
Plant Railroad Booklet,
1887.

tank with the help of a windmill and
hydraulic ram. From there the water was
conveyed to all parts of the grove by
underground pipes.

The return trip, heading toward Jacksonville at night, was unforgettable. By
the 1890s a powerful electric searchlight
highlighted the softly rounded orange
trees, the tree limbs with startled birds,
the sentimental couples in shaded nooks,
the leafy background, and green and
white cottages in tiny settlements. All
made a dramatic stage setting along the
river's edge.

In retrospect, the river steamers
provided a rich heritage of legendary figures and nostalgic memories for those
who traveled America's unusual, north-
flowing river. ■

Steamer *Osceola*, Lower Landing, Silver Springs, c. 1880.

The H.L. Hart steamer *Osceola* brought ex-President Grant up the Ocklawaha when he toured Silver Springs and Ocala in 1880.

According to a tourist of 1874, a journey up the Ocklawaha was "as fashionable as a promenade on the Rhine, and really more interesting and amusing."[1]

The Ocklawaha region remained unexplored until about 1867, its course as twisted as the strands of a rope with turns so frequent as to barely allow passage of a boat. Long poles were often used to keep from running ashore. The river's flow of some three hundred miles produced scenery that Northern travelers, who had spent their lives in well-ordered small towns and cities would long remember for its strange beauty.

After being photographed at the landing by a local artist, passengers boarded the little Ocklawaha steamer which departed from Palatka at 10 A.M. Accommodations had to be made in advance by

Post office at Sharpe's Ferry, c. 1875. Photograph by Jerome N. Wilson.

"In the vicinity of the alligator's nest we came upon a primitive post-office, consisting of a cigar box nailed upon the face of an old cypress-tree. It was sort of a central point for swampers, where they left their soiled notes and crooked writing to be conveyed to the places of destination by 'whomever came along.'" (From a Florida guide book, 1876.)

"An alligator in its natural habitat," c. 1898. Photograph by Underwood & Underwood.

"The practice of shooting from steamers at alligators, birds, etc., is one that should be speedily abandoned. Besides there are so many of the 'gallant sportsmen' who are careless in the use of their firearms, that they are constantly endangering the lives and persons of their fellow passengers." (From an article written by a tourist, 1876.) By 1890, shooting wildlife from the Silver Springs steamers was prohibited.

telegraph because twenty passengers was the usual quota. The steamers were built with two decks and a square wheelhouse high on the forward side. Rows of tiny staterooms—six-foot by three-foot shelves—were behind the second-story deck. A member of an 1875 excursion party told of the accommodations: "Our little steamer was full—nay, more than full; we fairly swarmed over her miniature decks, crowded her one cabin, and almost, I was about to say, hung on behind, so entirely did we fill every inch of her space. Every body heard what every body said; we dined in detachments, not being able to get into the cabin all at once; and when we were folded up on our shelves for the night, we could hear each other breathe all down the row."[2]

Another 1875 tourist wrote of the night journey: "That night I was wakened by a sharp blow on the little shuttered window....It was two o'clock....The river had grown very narrow, and as we passed the curves we seemed to be plunging into the thickets alongside, the bent tree branches making the sounds I had heard. We had come to the region of palms...below on the bushes bloomed a maze of flowers, standing out clearly for a moment as the light fell on them....Vines ran up the trees and [swung] downward in fantastic coils, and the air was heavy with fragrance. Every now and then a white crane flew up from the green thicket....Save the bird cries there was no sound. Onward we glided through the still forest, the light ever reddening in front and fading behind, like a series of wonderful dissolving views set up by some wizard of the wilderness."[3]

One interesting experience for tourists was passing another steamer at night. The little craft would claw its way close to the bank when a light and doleful sound signalled a distant boat. Around the curve she would come—her pitch-pine fires blazing high on the top, and the little deck

below crowded with passengers."[4] It was the custom for both sides to give a roaring shout to greet the event. Often, as the boats were passing, their respective black cooks, just inches apart, would exchange "whispered confidences from their little windows."[5]

Sometimes obstructions along the stream delayed travelers on the little steamers. An 1870 tourist told of a huge

fallen water oak blocking the channel. The captain of the craft and his crew had to use axes on the iron-hard wood, first chopping the limbs and then the great trunk. The work took hours, and some of the male passengers bravely waded in the black water of the swamp, getting wet to the waist. On land they came across a camp of two Florida crackers, who were gathering cypress for the manufacture of

When the Silver Springs steamers turned into the "run" from the muddy waters of the Ocklawaha, the transformation seemed magical: "So clear is the water that the bottom is distinctly visible everywhere. Thus we could see the fish both great and small, hundreds of turtles, and a great variety of marine plants as plainly as if they were at the surface."

The approach to Silver Springs, c. 1888. Photograph attributed to William H. Jackson.

"The 'spring' is said to have been discovered by Ponce de Leon, who imagined that he had found the 'fountain of youth' he had been so zealously seeking."

shingles. They found the men civil but pale, thin, and dull of intellect (a typical Northern reaction), but the campers' hut, the smouldering fire, and the deep forest background, presented a picture to the tourists not without a certain charm.

The Ocklawaha was a favorite trip for naturalists, who could be seen on deck with tiny nets catching flying insects. (Visitors were advised to make the trip early in the season because of the numerous fleas and mosquitos.) The river teemed with a great variety of fish, rare and curious; alligators were countless and gigantic turtles weighed up to five hundred pounds. Bird fanciers found it a paradise with the mockingbird in great numbers, parakeets, white and pink curlews, and many other birds of beautiful plumage. Mockingbirds were popular in Jacksonville and sold, in 1875, at prices from ten to fifty dollars. Birds that could imitate nearly every sound distinctly brought from one hundred to five hundred dollars.

Visitors leaving Palatka at 10 A.M. reached the Silver Springs "run" the next

The steamer *Astatula*, Ocklawaha River, 1893. Photograph by Jonas G. Mangold.

"A clear patch of the sky is seen, and the bright light of a summer evening is tossing the feathery crowns of the old cypress trees into a nimbus of glory, while innumerable paraquets, alarmed at our intrusion, scream out their fierce indignation, and then, flying away flash upon our admiring eyes their green and golden plumage." (From a tourist's notebook; written near sundown on the river.)

Cypress swamp, Ocklawaha River, c. 1888. Photograph attributed to William H. Jackson.

"As daylight increased, we found we were passing through a dense cypress-swamp, and that the channel selected had no banks but was indicated by blazed marks on the trunks of the towering trees." From *Appleton's Journal*, 1870.

morning, a trip of some one hundred miles from the mouth of the river. After leaving the Ocklawaha, the run to the famous spring was eight miles. The stream had a rapid current, and at a depth of twenty feet the bottom was clearly visible. The "fairy lakelet" was surrounded by beautiful tropical foliage, palms and moss-draped live-oak trees, wild grapevines and yellow jasmine, and solid banks of Cherokee roses.

On reaching the spring, travelers found it to be an almost circular basin about 125 feet wide and about forty feet at the greatest depth. The town of Silver Springs was not large in 1875, with a small hotel, two stores, and a half-dozen dwellings.

During a wait of several hours at Silver Springs, one excursion party secured light canoes and had lunch at a shady spot along the shore of the lake. Miraculously, a member of the party, a wealthy yachtsman from New York, produced tiny sandwiches and little cakes, served with champagne on ice! After dining, the party explored the center of the lake and experienced a feeling of floating in mid-space because the water was so clear that a pin could be seen on the bottom—"The trees were reflected like realities...with the prism-tinted fringes everywhere along the bottom, it was enchantment."[6]

Many visitors took the stage to Ocala, five miles away, traveling through rolling pine woods and hummocks to the neat little town. In 1869, the two hotels in town charged $1.50 a day or $25.00 a month, and several boarding houses welcomed travelers. The village also had two newspapers, a livery stable, a doctor, several churches, and a tri-weekly stage to Gainesville.

The Ocklawaha was impassable beyond Silver Springs until 1867. The hazard had been sunken logs, overhanging limbs, and the presence of floating islands. These were composed of curious aquatic plants which gathered floating grass and mud after becoming detached from the river

Silver Springs, c. 1877. Photograph by Charles Bierstadt.

A tourist in 1876 recounted: "Finally we reached the spring, an almost circular basin. Here we made a landing and a stay of three hours. The trees and plants were reflected with the most minute fidelity. There are several springs in different parts of the basin and at the spring where the greatest quantity of water flows, the upward current is strong enough to carry a large stone a distance of twenty-five feet. When going over it in a small boat it seems as if you were suspended in mid-air—the boat and its occupants being reflected in the depths of the clear water."

Steamer *Marion*, Captain Gray, Iola Landing, Ocklawaha River, c. 1875. Photograph by Jerome N. Wilson.

Sidney Lanier later described sleeping aboard the *Marion*, after visiting Silver Springs in 1874: "And then it was bed-time. Let me tell you how to sleep on an Ocklawaha steamer in May. With a small bribe persuade Jim, the steward, to take a mattress out of your berth and lay it slanting just along the railing that encloses the lower part of the deck, in front, and to the left, of the pilot-house. Lie flat-backed down on the same, draw your blanket over you, put your cap on your head in consideration of the night air, fold your arms, say a little prayer or other and fall asleep with a star looking right down your eye. When you awake in the morning…you will feel as new as Adam."

bottom. They had to be cut into pieces with crosscut saws before removal from the channel. Once the river was cleared, small tourist steamers could run with some regularity to Lake Griffin, Lake Eustis, and through the narrows to Lake Harris, ending at Lake Dunham and the tiny village of Ocklawaha.

The return trip from Silver Springs was much faster by some four or five hours. Passengers traveling the morning steamer reached Palatka about four o'clock the following morning, where connections could be made for a steamer bound for Jacksonville, despite the early hour.

Late in the afternoon the steamer reached the narrowest part of the river where a vessel would have only inches to spare if it measured any more than twenty-one feet across. By nightfall the steamer arrived at Orange Springs, the point where the Ocklawaha turned and

Silver Springs Hotel, 1886. Photograph by Stanley J. Morrow.

This out-of-the-way hotel at Silver Springs was a resort representing a large financial venture. On January 25, 1886, the awaiting public was notified of its opening—complete with gas lights and electric bells. For the pleasure seeker it offered fine orchestral music, a new pavilion, boating, and billiards.

Town Hall (and probably the post office), Silver Springs, c. 1873. Photograph by E. & H.T. Anthony.

flowed eastward and Orange Creek ran westward. The town was often a stopover for steamboat passengers to or from Silver Springs, especially in the early days of tourist travel before the Civil War.

The landing was about a mile from the sulphur spring where a boarding house had received guests after 1843. By 1851 it had become a popular resort for invalids and a summertime watering place for plantation owners from east Florida. The spa became popular once again in the mid-1880s with the opening of a few small hotels and a new wharf. Railroads bypassed the town, and as the era of the steamboat faded, Orange Springs fell into obscurity.

One excursion party visited Orange Springs during daylight hours, after making arrangements with the captain of the steamer to wait while they took a mail pole-barge into the wild creek. They visited Orange Lake, where orange groves extended back for miles. Once ashore, they had iced orangeade with an orange

The *Okahumkee*, Captain Rise, Ft. Brooke, Ocklawaha, April 17, 1876. Photograph by Jerome N. Wilson and O. Pierre Havens.

The landing was about two miles from Orange Spring and had a sulphur spring "with strongly impregnated waters." No accommodations were available.

blossom floating in each glass. The party drank to the bold, legendary Ocklawaha Indian warrior Hallak Tustenugge.

After leaving Orange Springs, the steamer passed an interesting landing called Fort Brooke (one of three forts of the same name in Florida), the site of an Indian attack in March of 1841. In conversation with people at landings along the way, travelers found that most of the settlers and small plantation owners had been well-to-do before the war but were satisfied in their new wilderness homes.

A trip along the Ocklawaha remained the "chief sensational feature of a tour in Florida" well into the 1890s. By then tourists could take a steamer to Silver Springs and return to Palatka by train. Travelers could also take the rail from Tampa, then go by steamer on the Ocklawaha to Palatka. One 1893 tourist recalled: "Nothing that Florida offers in the ordinary route of travel approaches the horrible fascination of a night ride through this semi-tropical swamp. It is something to talk over by the home fireside."[7] ■

In 1852, *Winter from Home* advised tourists: "We were told that Lake Monroe was a beautiful spot, somewhat frequented by strangers, but with insufficient accommodations. A small steamer visits it once a week, but the most desirable mode of reaching it, by persons traveling for pleasure, is to take an open boat, well provisioned, and properly manned, and encamp at night on the shores. By traveling in this mode, you can proceed to other lakes beyond Monroe, and if partial to fishing and gunning, you will have ample amusement on your voyage."

The small steamer was the *Darlington*, which made weekly trips to Enterprise. Fort Mellon, called Mellonville in 1852, was where civilization stopped; it was the dividing point for Florida's dense, little explored, and mysterious regions to the east, south, and west. The Indian River lay to the east, westward was the land of unchartered lakes, and to the south was the sparsely settled area around Orlando.

A great wilderness of water south of Orlando remained, a highway of lakes: Tohopekaliga, Cypress, and Kissimmee. And further along the Kissimmee River, Lake Okeechobee was largely the domain of the Seminole, his remaining paradise and happy hunting ground.

Such was the wilderness of great Lake Okeechobee and the area surrounding it in the early 1870s. Information about the lake was vague and often tinged with the romance of an unexplored country. Sensational tales were told about ruins of castles and monasteries with carved ornamental pillars and pirate dens containing untold treasure on a cypress island somewhere in the great lake. Other stories told of monkeys and baboons cavorting about in delightful groves of tropical fruits, where resided, much to the horror of listeners, spiders of four-pound weight.

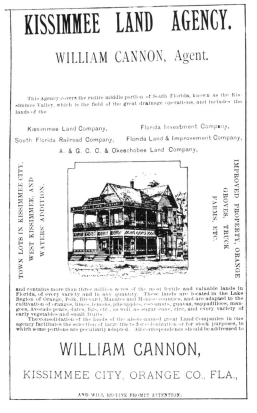

Advertisement. From South Florida Railroad brochure, 1887.

Mellonville from the wharf, c. 1880.

Sidney Lanier wrote of the town after visiting it in 1875: "…a neighborhood which is beginning to exhibit much activity in settlement and improvement. It has two hotels. Hereabouts are many orange-groves, and in the neighborhood are Sanford (where there is a money-order post-office, a sanitarium, "The Onoro Hotel"—etc.)." Mellonville, on Lake Monroe, was an early gateway to the east, south, and west.

Kissimmee City Bank, Kissimmee, c. 1886.

When Kirk Monroe, on his famous canoe trip, arrived in Kissimmee on February 27, 1882, he wrote in his diary: "Very like a western town. 20 houses, 2 saw mills running night and day. Left at 2 o'clock with a mule team for Orlando."

A tourist who visited the lake in 1872 (probably the only one brave enough in that year) said that the alligators were different. He recounted: "Shoals of alligators swarm up, their black heads dotting the water like water-worn pineknots. They rubbed their noses against the boat, and grunted loudly and deeply—a welcome, perhaps, though we viewed it in the light of a welcome addition to their bill-of-fare."[1]

By the early 1880s, the mystic curtain of Lake Okeechobee had disappeared. Hamilton Disston, the tool tycoon from Philadelphia, appeared on the scene. He pictured the area south of Orlando as a utopia for tourists and Kissimmee as the future tourist capital of Florida. He envisioned steamers leaving the town crowded with sightseers heading southward on a series of lakes connected by canals to the Kissimmee River and Lake Okeechobee. After a scenic tour of the lake, the cruise-steamer would turn westward over the canal-improved Caloosahatchee River and down to the Gulf wilderness at Punta Rassa, then northward to Punta Gorda or Tampa from where the grand tour would end with a rail trip back to Kissimmee.

Disston also dreamed of a canal to run eastward from Lake Okeechobee to the Atlantic Ocean, after the Caloosahatchee River had been dredged—a trans-Florida ship canal. His followers let it be known

that plans were in progress for large steamships coming in from New Orleans, en route to New York, to use the waterway which would give tourists a picturesque trip through the wild Everglades. However, these dreams did not come to fruition.

Meanwhile, by 1885 Kissimmee had the appearance of a charming little city destined for a bright future. Kerosene lamps, set on wooden poles, lined Main Street and Broadway. Their tender carried a little ladder as he performed his nightly duty. The townspeople said that their lamps were always clear and burning. The price of land rose some six hundred percent—only the beginning, they said.

Accommodations for the tourist were not overlooked. The Tropical Hotel, with space for 125 guests, fronted on the clear waters of Lake Tohopekaliga, surrounded by graceful lawns and tall pines. From its lofty observatory, visitors saw a panorama of the lake with vivid colors of water, sky, and vegetation. Rates were a little higher than elsewhere at three to four dollars a day, but then again, the rooms were large, handsomely furnished, and the hotel's epicurean cuisine was a delight. Four steamers toured Lake Tohopekaliga, and sailboats, steam yachts, and rowboats were available for excursions to the many idyllic picnic sites.

Elsewhere in central Florida, winter visitors came in great numbers during the 1880s. The South Florida Railroad began running trains to Orlando from Sanford's steamer docks in January of 1880, after President Grant had turned the first shovel of dirt in a gala celebration. Resort towns mushroomed along the railroad's right-of-way. One of the first was Altamonte Springs, "chiefly the resort of a large number of well-to-do Eastern and Northern men of business, who come for the perfect repose and quiet they get here."[2] The Altamonte Hotel, the town's finest, advertised the Springs as a healthy

place for curing dyspepsia and rheumatic catarrhal conditions resulting from pulmonary and bronchial diseases and "last but not least, the purest spring water that anywhere flows from the ground."[3] The hotel also claimed to be the center for alligator hunts.

Whatever title to tranquility the town may have held was shattered when the "Southern" branch of the Grand Army of the Republic circle held a most elegant affair to honor Mrs. Ulysses S. Grant at the hotel on March 30, 1893. For the festive occasion, the hotel was decorated with bunting, flags, and flowers. As the night progressed, the halls resounded with nostalgic revelry created by General Grant's whiskey-drinking former com-

rades-in-arms.

The next place of interest on the rail line between Altamonte Springs and Orlando in 1885 was the burgeoning town of Winter Park, destined to be the most fashionable town in all of central Florida. Two elements were needed for a successful resort, wealthy backers and a convenient railroad. Winter Park had both. A number of affluent businessmen, including a banker from Minneapolis and Colonel Fairbanks, the weighing-scale tycoon, pooled enough capital to build the largest luxury hotel south of St. Augustine.

The Seminole Hotel, first class in every way and *the* resort for Florida tourists, opened on January 1, 1886, with a

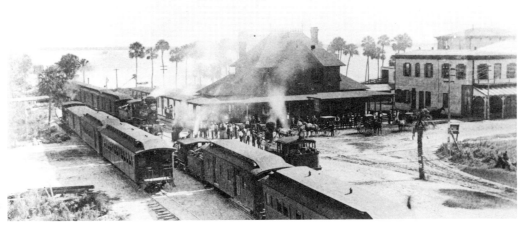

selected guest list of some four hundred people. Before the season was over some 2,300 guests had registered, and many more were turned away. The opening day had been skillfully heralded. Special trains brought in about three thousand socially acceptable people to inspect the hotel prior to New Year's Day.

For the tourist inclined to judge others by intellectual achievements rather than money, Winter Park had something to offer: the new Rollins College, an impeccable college with an impeccable enrollment. Orange City, over on the St. Johns River, and Winter Park had competed for the proposed college, and Winter Park emerged the winner in 1885. The *South Florida Times*, an Orange City newspaper wrote (with ill-grace): "Winter Park is a place surrounded by swamps, and about nine months out of the year the hooting owls hoot to the few families that will forever be the only inhabitants of Winter Park."

Americans had a long tradition for venerating the places where political leaders

Waiting for the train. Altamonte Springs, 1886. Photograph by Stanley J. Morrow.
The horse car ran from the station to the Altamonte Hotel, about a half-mile distant. During the summer months, the hotel's manager went north to operate the Twin Mountain House in the White Mountains of New Hampshire.

South Florida Railroad, near Orlando, 1886. Photograph by Stanley J. Morrow.

The main line of the South Florida ran between Sanford and Tampa, after 1884, with a branch line to Bartow connecting with the Florida Southern Railroad to Punta Gorda and the fishing paradise of the southwest coast.

Boat House, the Seminole Hotel, Lake Osceola, Winter Park, 1886. Photograph by Stanley J. Morrow.

To provide recreation for its guests, the hotel had croquet grounds, a tennis court, billiard room, bowling alley, good saddle and driving horses, fishing tackle, rowboats, sailboats, two steam yachts, and, for further relaxation, an orchestra for dancing or just listening.

had stayed, and Winter Park had a generous share of famous names on its roster. President Arthur had pronounced the town the prettiest spot he had seen in Florida. In 1889 President Cleveland ventured into Winter Park, an oasis of political opposition where the Republicans outnumbered the Democrats two to one. However, his reception was polite and cordial, and when his party reached the Seminole Hotel, he found an elegant repast spread out amid floral decorations, a pleasant surprise for the hungry travelers. Robert Howe, operator of the Orlando Ice Works (presumably a Democrat), had sent a beautiful wreath frozen in the center of a cake of ice.

President and Mrs. Harrison visited Winter Park in 1890. They had traveled in regal style aboard Henry M. Flagler's private railroad car, which had been attached to the rear end of the West India Mail Express. The party included Vice-President Morton, his wife, and others, and all were warmly received.

What did Winter Park look like in 1890? A tourist wrote: "On leaving the train the traveler at once notes an air of neatness and thrift in streets, houses and stores. Elsewhere are charming cottages, often overlooking one or another of the several lakes. Well-laid board walks are a pleasant

Advertisement. From Plant Railroad brochure, 1887.

The Hotel Seminole, Winter Park, 1886. Photograph by Stanley J. Morrow.

The hotel opened on New Year's night in 1886. Light sparkled from hundreds of gas jets and bonfires blazed on the lawns. Many prominent winter guests came to fill the rooms and to celebrate the hotel's debut. They promenaded in the many corridors and piazzas, dined on the best of cuisines, and danced in the gala ballroom.

relief from the deep sand often encountered, and convenient tramways afford facilities for those who would rather ride than walk. From the observatory atop the Seminole Hotel fourteen lakes can be seen. Within easy driving distance is *Clay Spring*, across which strong swimmers strive in vain to pass, so powerful is the upward rush of water through a dark chasm in the rock."[4] By 1893, Winter Park was known everywhere for its gay and fashionable society and its balmy air. The Hotel Seminole made a proud boast "that more millionaires and beauties were gathered on its piazzas than any other like space in Florida."[5]

Orlando was the next stop on the South Florida Railroad, about four miles beyond the Winter Park station. It was said, in 1886, that when a train drew into the handsome depot, a hullabaloo broke forth amidst a frenzy of Negro hotel drummers, shouting the excellence of their respective establishments. The town was called "The Phenomenal City" in 1886, and its creation and growth was due to the individual enterprise of its private citizens. The town appealed to the passing tourist because of its beautiful orange groves and its sixteen lakes. Orlando, they said, "is built on the peel of the orange." It had a commercial air, and traveling salesmen, rather than tourists, filled its hotels. A shopping center for those living for miles around, it had a large number of stores which sold a wide variety of items.

The best way for winter visitors to spend a season in Orlando was to rent a cottage and buy food from local shops rather than dine in expensive restaurants. Living was cheap when compared to elsewhere in the state. Prices in 1884 were: flour, half-barrel, $4.25; coffee, 20¢ a pound; three-pound can of apricots, 35¢; ginghams, 11¢ a yard; men's shoes, $1.00 a pair; and straw hats, 25¢ and up.

The city's first step toward entertainment and culture came in 1884 with the

The Seminole Hotel launch, the *Fanny Knowles*, Lake Osceola, Winter Park, 1886. Photograph by Stanley J. Morrow.

"Last Saturday A.M. the last stump was blown out of the canal....The *Fanny Knowles* was steamed up and with Commodore Paige at the wheel started on her first trip into Lake Virginia....We were royally received on that side by the ringing of the college bells, cheers of students and residents." From *The Lochmede*, 1887. The launch made two trips daily around the lakes, fare was twenty-five cents—"a very pleasant excursion."

Winter Park, view towards the South Florida Railroad, 1886. Photograph by Stanley J. Morrow.

When President Grover Cleveland visited Winter Park in 1889, he took a tourist's outing on the "bounding horse car" pulled by a pampered old mule—Cleveland weighed 260 pounds.

Orange County Fair, looking towards Lake Eola from the roof of Exhibition Hall, February, 1887. Photograph by Stanley J. Morrow.

The photography tent, with its open-roof skylight, was probably operated by L.H. Geer, who had a studio on Church street, Orlando. The race track grandstand faces the lake.

opening of the opera house on Court Street. Miss Emma Thursby, the grand opera star, was the first singer. In 1890, a more rugged type of entertainment came to town. "Wild Jim," just in from the Wild West, gave an exhibition of horsemanship and showed his skill with a rifle, making a bull's-eye every time he shot at small glass balls, marbles, and walnuts. A few years later John Prang, a local man and collector of wildlife—birds, snakes, coons, and foxes—opened a menagerie in downtown Orlando. He charged twenty-five cents for a lecture on wildlife. Some of his lectures were better than others. If he had been drinking in the next-door saloon just before the opening show, he would reach in the rattlesnake cage and, with a shaky hand, pull out a rattler for a closer view by the audience.

Tourists liked to take home tales of incredible things, large and small, that they had seen. Out on Lake Concord, a grove specialized in navel oranges, and on display was a prize-winning specimen which weighed some three and one-quarter pounds and measured eighteen inches around the outside. Eventually a mammoth photograph of the orange replaced the original.

Winter visitors coming to Florida for the first time were curious about how Christmas was celebrated in a warm climate—a climate, had they stopped to think about it, not unlike that of Palestine. But did it seem like Christmas? One answer came from a lady tourist in 1891: "First and best of all...the temperature was high...80 in the shade and a brisk breeze was stirring throughout the day. The woods were melodious with the songs of birds. The front yards were bright and lovely with roses...and many other flowers....Show-windows of many stores were made conspicuous with fireworks and firecrackers, etc.; and on

"Cracker Day." Orange Avenue, Orlando, c. 1886. Photograph by Stanley J. Morrow.

Every Saturday was "Cracker Day" in Orlando. It was the day when farmers and country people came to do their shopping and watch Bud Yates wrestle his pet alligator in front of Sinclair's real estate office and Alligator John's curio store. To amuse the crowd, he would hold the alligator's mouth open and let the people look down its throat.

Christmas Day the small boys—white and black—were discharging firecrackers, toy-pistols, etc., almost incessantly. At night there were many fine displays of fireworks by private parties. Indeed it seemed more like a Fourth of July celebration than Christmas."[6]

By 1886, Orlando had a new railroad, The Tavares, Orlando and Atlantic Railway, for those wishing to visit the lake country. Two trains a day ran from what was probably the least pretentious depot in the entire country, an old boxcar placed on a siding in downtown Orlando. Tavares, along the west shore of Lake Dora, was the point where five separate railroads came together by 1889. Also a local steamer stopped at points on lakes Eustis, Harris, and Griffin, before going on to the Ocklawaha River, passing Silver Springs before reaching the St. Johns River. For the rail traveler, trains departing Tavares went northeastward across the St. Johns River, connecting with the main line of the Jacksonville, Tampa and Key West Railroad, just south of Seville.

George Barbour, author and reporter, who toured the large lakes, in 1880 wrote: "A trip upon them enables the tourist to see some of the most striking and picturesque scenery in the state. Just south of Lake Eustis lies Lake Dora, another large lake, whose high and blufflike shores reminds one rather of the lake region of western New York than the low and sandy levels that usually characterize Florida."[7] When Barbour made his observation, he was standing on the high ground of the future town of Mount Dora, where settlers within a few years would beautify their avenues with rows of live oak trees.

Scene on Lake Dora, at Tavares, c. 1900.

A roundabout boat tour of the lakes—Dora, Eustis, Harris, and Griffin—all connected by canals, was the best and easiest way to see the lake country.

Lake Eustis Park, picnic, c. 1885. Photograph by C.T. Smith.

Almost every town in central Florida had a *Cornet* brass band. They dressed in cadet gray with epaulets and shiny brass buttons, and the many bands vied with one another in musical competitions.

On returning to Sanford, about twenty-five miles east of Tavares, an 1890 sightseer could transfer to the Lake Charm train. The small train traveled southeastward, passing a series of orange groves which resembled a dark evergreen tunnel. One tourist said that when the train went by Lake Jessup, he saw a half-dozen lean, bone-picked cows, but the scene changed when he came to the town of Oviedo with its bright red warehouse and handsome depot. Next came Lake Charm nestling in the middle of a soft green sward set in beautiful live oaks—the seat of Clifton Springs. The visitor now at the end of his tour of central Florida could see beyond the station a pretty panorama of vine-covered cottages, villas, orange groves, and a thriving vineyard—a pleasant ending to an interesting journey. ■

Street view, Sanford, 1896. Photograph by Jesse S. Wooley.

"This is a street scene in Sanford which formerly was a very lucky town being the distribution point for all freight for southern central Fla. Also the shipping point of many orange growers in this section. But now you may find block after block of empty stores and the town has a half deserted appearance and as one man said resembles a Kansas 'Boom Town' after the boom has left." (From Wooley's travelogue.)

A morning's catch, 1875. Photograph by G.R. Kidder.

It was an important day for the west coast of Florida when the railroad line from Fernandina to Cedar Keys was completed just before the opening guns of the Civil War. The little settlements dotting the coastline could now be reached more quickly from the northeast by making a voyage from New York to Fernandina, taking a train to Cedar Keys, and then boarding a steamer to ports along the Gulf.

However, the new travel route was short-lived because of a wartime blockade along the Florida coast. After the war was over, the train resumed its run, and the adventuresome tourist or settler began exploring a land for which it was not possible to obtain books or accurate maps, a wild region with forests, rivers, white sandy coasts, and only a few settlements, scattered far and wide.

Instead of going by the Cedar Keys route to the west coast, the tourist could leave the train at Gainesville and continue by stage to Tampa, a two-day, one-night trip of 134 miles, an experience never to be forgotten. The coach was a four-horse affair, heavy and lumbering, built to travel over the white sandy road. Passengers had to hold up their feet when fording a stream, and they also had to keep an eye on the baggage atop the coach in case it was jolted from the rack. The driver, known as "Old Man Roper," was famous for the handling of his long snake whip and his salty vocabulary. Passengers found it fascinating to watch him leap from the coach to catch gophers, which he later sold for twenty-five cents each.

In Tampa, situated on the east bank of the Hillsborough River at the upper end of Tampa Bay, the traveler of 1869 found two hotels, the Florida House and the Orange Grove Hotel. Both charged two dollars a day. About thirty miles further

Scene at Palmetto Beach, Tampa, c. 1900.

Lighthouse on Egmont Key, c. 1865. Sketch by Alfred A. Waud.

The lighthouse, built during the Seminole War, was badly damaged during the 1848 hurricane, and rebuilt at the cost of $16,000. Egmont Key was a land base for the blockading squad- ron during the Civil War, and several buildings were erected near the lighthouse. Many Union families found refuge from the mainland on the key and lived there until they could take passage on ships bound for Key West or the North.

south stood a lighthouse on Egmont Key at the south entrance to Tampa Bay harbor, an area said to have been a landing place of early Spanish explorers.

Not far from Egmont Key were small isolated settlements about six miles in from the mouth of the Manatee River. A weekly mail boat from Tampa kept the settlers informed about local and national news. A favorite area for sportsmen, the settlement of Manatee was very pretty with orange, lemon, and banana trees. Beyond the cultivation were the hummocks—almost impenetrable jungles where lay "wild beasts, reptiles, insects, and innumerable birds, some of brilliant plumage and beautiful song, while the rivers and estuaries teem with fish."[1]

The hotel keeper in Manatee, Josiah Gates, known as Judge Gates, moved to the community in 1842. At first a log house accommodated guests, and later, in the 1850s, he built a new twenty-room frame hotel featuring an underground cistern for water brought into the kitchen through wooden pipes.

It was to this primitive land that Sir St. George Gore, celebrated English sportsman, came to hunt. He brought a large number of servants, horses, hounds, and other equipment. Another party of English sportsmen coming to Manatee in 1874 were advised by Sir Gore that game

Mouth of the Hillsborough River, Tampa, c. 1885.

Rear view, Villa Zanza or Adams' Castle, Braidenton (Bradenton), c. 1900.

The "castle" was built by Major Alden Adams in about 1881-1882. Steps led to the front and rear piazzas. A number of basement rooms opened onto the ground, and vines hid them from view giving a rather mysterious appearance. The grounds were beautiful with footpaths and drives of oyster shells leading from the castle to an open road lined with orange trees, rare plants, and exotic flowering shrubs. Adams was a bird fancier and gathered together a rare collection of birds from many tropical countries.

was abundant and that the group should start southward into the interior for Myakka Lake. After securing an oxen team, wagons, horses, camping equipment, and a suitable guide, the party began its journey through the hummocks and swamps into bleak prairie land with a sandy track. Travel was difficult deep in the wilderness, and the party stopped often to clear fallen trunks and brush. They passed swampy ponds with vari-colored water lilies and great cranes standing by with graceful elegance.

On their first day's journey, the campers met with a rough-looking group of three Florida crackers, armed with rifles and revolvers, followed by two hounds as savage looking as their masters. After dogs in both parties growled, the men exchanged a quiet salutation. One of the Englishmen described the crackers as men only met with in the wild, some "ne'er-do-wells" of the settlements or criminals hiding from justice.

An isolated plantation near upper Myakka Lake provided shelter for the party during their stay. One of their excursions was a hog-hunting party accompanied by several magnificent Cuban bloodhounds, descendants of the animals formerly used to track runaway slaves. During the chase, one of the party was standing in thick palmetto-scrub up to his waist when an ocelot sprang toward him; his second shot felled the beautiful animal, which measured over four feet from nose to tail.

The party also made canoe trips along the Myakka River, through murky swamps, and finally into the bay to a settlement called Hickory Bluff, on Peace Creek near Charlotte Harbor. When hearing that a small schooner was loading for Key West, the party decided to take passage to Punta Rassa on the Caloosahatchee River, some distance south of Charlotte Harbor. About sunset they passed an island called Carrabo Key, on

The *Kissimmee* at Braidenton (Bradenton) Dock, c. 1885.

The *Kissimmee* brought passengers and freight across the Manatee River to the village of Palmetto, making three trips daily.

which lived an Englishman, Captain Jocelyn, who was said to have been the terror of the whole coast—a bloodthirsty pirate and murderer. Many strangers lured to his island were never heard of again. On being questioned, Jocelyn invariably answered that the man was knocked overboard by the mainsail and drowned. One of the sportsmen met the desperado at the telegraph station at Punta Rassa, and described him as a man between forty-five and fifty-five, of medium height, with flashing black eyes and heavy eyebrows, wearing a flannel shirt, ragged pants tucked into long sea-boots, a red leather belt about the waist containing a revolver and long knife, and he carried a rusty old rifle which never left his hands.

In contrast to the English party who found their steamer from Cedar Keys to be rickety and dirty, an American group,

A Florida hunting party, c. 1883. Photograph attributed to Alonzo G. Grant.

City Dock and lower Main Street, looking north. Belle Haven Inn on right. Sarasota, 1888. Photograph attributed to Felix Pinard.

the year before, had found their steamer *Emilie* an excellent and comfortable sea-boat, which made weekly trips with stops along the coast. The party's boat, shipped from the north, was waiting at Manatee for an expedition down to Little Gasparilla Pass and other popular hunting and fishing grounds.

In 1885 an English tourist who had taken a mail coach from Tampa to Bartow, a town of three hundred inhabitants, published an interesting account: "The ride, or rather walk, through the sandy track from Tampa had lasted fifteen hours…a continuous, bruising, bone-disjointing, jerking, temper-trying jaunt of forty miles…passing many an acre of rich orange-orchards…fields of sugar-cane, ready for the mill, and acres and acres of land from which the pines had been burnt…awaiting the time when the settler shall put his axe to their roots.…We had to provision ourselves beforehand—eating our late breakfast and early dinner out of the polished tins our good hotel-manager had provided."[2]

The owner of Blount's Hotel at Bartow, along with a party of ten, met the mail stage and, with an oil lamp in hand, greeted the boarders for his hotel. The landlord brought the Englishman into the "saloon," a room with two long tables and a number of chairs. A supper awaited—cold steak, cold tinned-beef and cold cab-

bage, everything cold except the steaming coffee. Everyone in the party gathered round in a picturesque group to watch the new guest busy with knife and fork. As for bed, the Englishman felt if he were to spend two dollars for accommodations he wanted a bed for himself and clean sheets. A Kentuckian who had paid only a dollar was put in with a Texan who grumbled. The bedroom was interesting with

Barn party. Unidentified location, July 4, c. 1872.

Barn dances were a popular amusement in Florida. The rafters were decorated with native mosses or grasses, and lanterns made a romantic setting for lively couples dancing to music from fiddles and harmonicas. Refreshments were provided for all ages.

Picnic scene. Eagle Lake, c. 1885. Photograph by Stanley J. Morrow.

Eagle Lake was a favorite spot for picnics, both large and small, especially after a branch rail line ran south to Bartow. In 1887, more than three hundred Bartow residents, coming in by train, met with groups from Punta Gorda and Charlotte Harbor for a huge Sunday School picnic.

plenty of lumber. Bookshelves held *Washington Reports* and schoolbooks. But the thing that caught the attention of the Englishman was the stuffed wildcat on a wooden perch over the bedstead: "I found that the moon gradually got up in the night and shone on the wild cat's eyes."[3]

The English traveler found Bartow to be a charming little settlement cut out of the forest. One humorous scene was watching "seven of the inmates of Blount House careening up and down on roller skates in a most ungainly fashion—four young women (ages from sixteen to forty) and three young men (one an Italian, whose effusive courtesies were positive nectar to the American ladies)."[4] He also noted land agents and attorneys looking in at the hotel for orders before they left in buggies to inspect land within twenty miles around Bartow. Halcyon days were at hand, for the railroad would reach the little town in January, 1885, just three months after the Englishman's visit.

As the network of railroad lines penetrated southward and westward during the 1880s and 1890s, travel to hitherto remote areas became possible. The west coast owed much of its development to Henry Bradley Plant, the great railroad and steamship entrepreneur. He would transform Tampa into an important city, and he would also be responsible for the settlement and prosperity of a multitude of little towns springing up everywhere along the many branched rail lines. The building of luxury hotels at strategic travel points was part of the Plant enterprise to insure a profitable tourist industry. Before the Civil War, Plant, an official with the famous Adams Express Company, had been in charge of the Southern states. Many Florida and Georgia railroads became bankrupt and Plant, with other associates, bought up controlling interests in several lines. By 1882 his railroads extended down into Florida. The Plant system included Tampa and many points

Advertisement. South Florida Railroad brochure, 1887.

in the Central and Gulf regions of the state.

By the summer of 1886, passengers boarding the train at Jacksonville could reach Punta Gorda on the west coast in about twelve hours. Connections from there, by steamer, ran three times weekly to Punta Rassa, Fort Meyers, and other coastal ports. Following the arrival of a new rail route to Punta Gorda, the railroad company built a new hotel to accommodate five hundred people: "All the rooms are built on one side of the house, to command the water view. A long pier runs out from the hotel, off which all kinds of fish except Tarpon are taken in abundance."[5]

Sportsmen interested in tarpon fishing with rod and reel could take the local steamer *Alice Howard* for the five-hour trip to James City on the southern end of Pine Island, where they could stay at the San Carlos Hotel, which promised that "Ladies can accompany their husbands

"Ready to Gaff." 1889.

A tourist who came to Pine Island, near Punta Rassa, to fish for tarpon said that the largest one taken by rod and reel, was recorded on the score book at St. James City as weighing 184 pounds. (Engraving from *Scribner's Magazine*, 1889.)

and brothers without the risk of being otherwise than comfortable." A few miles distant at Punta Rassa, millionaire sportsmen found the famous Tarpon House primitive but comfortable and open all year. The Shultz Hotel was also favored by prominent sportsmen, including Grover Cleveland.

Punta Rassa, formerly Fort Dulany, was situated at the mouth of the Caloosahatchee River. The old fort building housed a telegraph station completed in 1869. The telegraph line from Jacksonville connected with a newly laid cable to Key West and Havana. Travelers could send a message home for $2.50, a valu-

San Carlos Hotel, St. James City, Pine Island, 1889.

The flourishing village of St. James City, at the southerly end of Pine Island, was a haven for enthusiastic tarpon fishermen. Tropical fruit trees and cocoanut plants were brought in to beautify the area for the pleasure of Northerners. (Engraving from *Scribner's Magazine*, 1889.)

The Hendry House, Fort Meyers, c. 1889. Photograph by J.A. Enseminger.

Francis A. Hendry, the cattle king of South Florida, moved to Fort Meyers in 1853. His son converted the house into a hotel after 1889. Only two hotels in town received guests in 1885, the year of Thomas Edison's first visit—the Braman and Keystone hotels.

Mirror Lake, Lakeland, from the Tremont House, c. 1892. Photograph by O. Pierre Havens.

"The little town is remarkable for its pure air and water, its accessibility and its excellent hotel. The 'Tremont' is known to every commercial traveler who traverses the State, and he manages to spend Sunday there if possible." The hotel opened on December 15, 1886, and was managed by Mr. Ives from the Metropolitan Hotel, Asbury Park, New Jersey.

able service in an isolated area.

A few miles up the Caloosahatchee River was the small town of Fort Meyers, visited by Thomas A. Edison in March of 1885. Edison had wintered in St. Augustine but found the climate too wet and cold, and before returning home had suggested to friends that a cruise on the Gulf might be pleasant. The party left Jacksonville by train for Cedar Keys, and from there the entourage sailed along the coast to Tampa, Sarasota Bay, Charlotte Harbor, and on to Fort Meyers. After his second marriage, in 1886, Fort Meyers became Edison's winter home. Other wealthy men also wintered in the beautiful little town, once a favorite of the Indians Osceola, Billy Bow-Legs, and Tiger Tail as a place of refuge during the Indian Wars. However, Fort Meyers still lacked a good hotel, and it needed better

facilities for crossing the river. A daily boat line to Punta Gorda took several hours, whereas a train would have taken but an hour.

Meanwhile, tourists en route to Tampa from Sanford or Orlando by rail enjoyed the scenery. One observer wrote: "Returning to Bartow Junction the road passes through a lovely wild scenery of lakes, made attractive by charming villa sites, by park-like open pines…or by green coverts of the deer, and where the slender cougar lies in wait for the doe."[6] Travelers soon passed Fitzhugh and reached Lakeland, at the junction of the two arms of the Plant system. The little town was known for its lakes, pure air, and excellent hotel. After Plant City, the ground sloped gradually by the suburban settlements of Seffner, Mango, and Orient, and the passenger arrived in Tampa.

The coming of the railroad to Tampa, in 1884, had a magical effect, and new hotels catering to tourists were built. On January 7, 1886, Plant brought into port a luxurious two-hundred-foot steamship to the delight of crowds who cheered the community's new benefactor. Plans for the Tampa Bay Hotel were underway, and the cornerstone was laid on July 26, 1888. Hundreds of craftsmen were brought in to build the opulent structure. A tourist of 1893 described the inn: "You see it as novel and imposing, and as of the purely 'moor-r-rish' style of architecture with

View of Sulphur Springs, near Tampa, c. 1900.

Above Tampa, on the Hillsborough river, is a Sulphur Spring thirty feet in diameter and twelve feet deep. The springs were opened to the public by Dr. J.H. Mills, who purchased the property in 1900. Before 1908, when a trolley line ran to the site, the springs could be reached only by horse and buggy or bicycle over a narrow rickety bridge.

Tampa Bay Hotel, 1891.

"The moorish arches, with graceful horseshoe curves everywhere....Thirteen marble columns support a balcony forming the second story. In public rooms paintings of late French school stand side by side with faded old masters. Everywhere mirrors in golden frames—antique and modern—massive doors in beveled glass leading to parlors, halls, libraries and writing rooms." The parlor was furnished with beautiful old antiques, and in the dining room the waiter brought "beef on a bit of French porcelain, your salad on an old Vienna plate, ice on a saucer designed by Moritz Fischer and coffee in a Wedgwood cup." The hotel, one of the finest resort hotels in the world, also offered a club house, large swimming pool, double bowling alley, and a shuffleboard room. (From *The Tatler*, 1893.)

domes and minarets and horseshoe arches."[7] The dining halls had every appointment, and suites of rooms furnished every comfort of a private mansion. The entire building was built for luxury—baths, electric lights, rich furnishings, and decorations—all in excellent taste. Although the hotel was completed early in 1890, the opening was delayed while Mrs. Plant was overseas looking for art objects, furniture, velvets, and other fine items—treasures which arrived in port by the shipload. Invitations to the opening went out all over the world. The affair took place February 5, 1891, and the finest of foods and wines were served to distinguished guests who danced to music provided by a New York orchestra. Onlookers said the event had the atmosphere of a huge house party.

Visitors now flocked to Tampa with its superb travel and hotel accommodations. The Tampa Bay Inn, a new Plant hotel, was built on pilings where the railroad connected with the steamship lines. A tourist of 1895 described the Inn: "A trestle is built out seven-eighths of a mile over the water where it is shallow, over which the train took us to the inn, a charming hotel with wide galleries half way around it. To look out of the windows one might imagine one's self on a steamer without the dreaded motion."[8]

From the Port of Tampa "may be seen the pretty village of St. Petersburg, which is located six miles away, near the southern extremity of the sub-peninsula that lies between the bay and the gulf. This is a clean, breezy, delightful resort for the tourist or invalid in winter. It is easily reached either by water or rail, and the well-equipped hotels offer welcome and the best of accommodations to visitors."[9] St. Petersburg had a long wharf where Havana steamers docked. The pier was popular with fishermen, and boats could be hired for a day's excursion down to Egmont Key, Manatee, and Sarasota Bay.

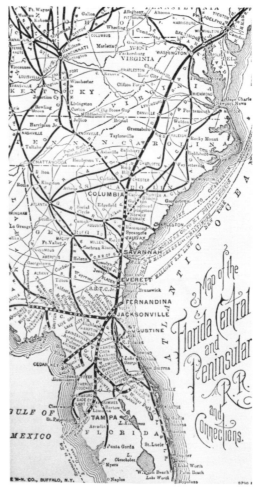

Central Avenue, St. Petersburg, c. 1905.

Tourists came to St. Petersburg in the 1890s either by steamer from Port Tampa or by the Orange Belt Railway, a ride said to have been a twenty-mile-per-hour jaunt with a rickety old engine. When the rail service was improved in the late 1890s, the town began to grow and prosper.

A few miles northwest of Tampa was the quaint town of Tarpon Springs, noted for its sponge industry. A brochure of 1896 described the town as a "bright, clear flowery town of one thousand inhabitants…nestled around the largest spring on the peninsula.…The waters here are wide enough and deep enough to float many vessels, and they flow gently down until they meet the waters of Anclote River, then into St. Joseph's Bay, some three miles distant, and thence to the Gulf."[10] The town had a large well-kept hotel and streets beautified with tropical trees and flower gardens.

A few miles south of Tarpon Springs was the little village of Dunedin. Clearwater, the next town south, was built on high ground on the line of the Orange Belt Railroad: "The approach from the depot is on a shelled street that leads due west to the brow of the bluff and thence down to the public dock. This street view of the harbor, the islands and the gulf beyond is truly enchanting.…The winter residents of Clearwater are chiefly from the South and West.…Bathing in the harbor or in the surf beyond is a daily sport, and almost every home upon the bluff has a bath house and a fishing hut far out in the water, with latticed walkways built upon piles by which to reach them.…The evening views from the verandas on the bluff

CLEARWATER FLORIDA

SEAVIEW HOTEL

Clearwater, Florida. From railroad brochure, c. 1896.

Clearwater's first hotel was the Orange Bluff, built in 1880. One of its first guests was Theodore Kamensky, a noted Russian sculptor whose work was inspired by contemporary life, notably "The First Step" and "Children in the Rain." Symbolic of liberty, his work caused him to leave Russia. He continued work as a sculptor but also built the Sea View Hotel (above) which overlooked the harbor. Other interesting characters found freedom along the water. One, an aged hermit who lived in an old fish-house, wrote poetry which he bestowed upon visitors.

are lovely beyond description. The sun
sinks down in the waters and sometimes
shows a double reflection upon their
glassy surface. The fleecy clouds assume
more beautiful colors than were ever
seen in Italy. The moonlight nights give a
charming finish to the days, and the
reflection of both moon and stars in the
clear water charms the sight."[11]

The beauty of Clearwater Harbor was
recognized by Henry Plant, and during
the summer of 1896, he began building
the Hotel Belleview. The hotel stood high
above the bay, and every room commanded a view of the water. The path
down to the landing was a series of ter-
races, parks, and avenues. The grand
opening took place on January 15, 1897,
and almost overnight the hotel was a success, catering to business tycoons and
railroad presidents, and other wealthy
visitors.

As the century drew to a close, people
of wealth and culture from all over the
country visited Florida's west coast, and
many found its beauty irresistible. ■

**The Belleview-Biltmore
Hotel, Belleair, 1895.**

**Construction began in 1895
on the four-story, three-
hundred-foot hotel, which
fronted on a high bluff
above the bay. After the
hotel's grand opening in**

**January 15, 1897, it quickly
became a favorite resort
with railroad presidents,
steel magnates, and other
tycoons. As many as fifteen
private railroad cars rested
at one time on the siding
by the hotel.**

9

Of all the resort towns in Florida, St. Augustine, fondly called the "Ancient City," was the earliest and most often visited by tourists. The city, protected from the ocean by the narrow island of Anastasia, emanated an old world charm with its Spanish architecture, its ruins, the scent of orange blossoms along the narrow streets, a siren's call which held the visitor enraptured for days or weeks.

After viewing the old Spanish fort San Marco, with its mysterious ancient bastions and towers, tourists became curious about the town's history and sought information from guide books or local historians. Until it came under American control in 1821, St. Augustine had been the scene of many bloody conflicts among nations or individuals seeking power and wealth.

Travel to the ancient city in the 1830s was usually by ship, and the approach from the ocean was guarded by breakers, as far as the eye could see. The channel was very narrow and often shifted during or after storms, and even though experienced local pilots were available to pole over the bar, vessels sometimes had to lie off the coast for days, a hardship for invalid travelers.

A lady visitor to the city reminisced in 1874: "Forty years ago the town was largely Spanish or Moorish in its architecture. The houses were all built of coquina, with a blank wall toward the north, galleries running around a courtyard behind, where were flowers, vines, and a central fountain. The halls with their stone arches, opened out into this greenery without doors of any kind, tropical fashion." She went on to say that these were proud days, the old families holding sway, the slaves well-treated, and hospitality boundless. In one old mansion, she writes, "We had our gay little parties, with wines, and those delicious curled-up

The City Gates, c. 1875. Photograph by the Florida Club.

"Turning into St. George Street, we found at the northern end of the town the old City Gates, the most picturesque ruin of picturesque St. Augustine. The two pillars are Moresque, surmounted by a carved pomegranate." (From *Harper's New Monthly Magazine*, 1874.)

cakes, all stamped with figures, thin as a wafer, crisp and brittle, which seemed to be peculiar to St. Augustine."[1]

In 1835, after Major Dade and his 107 comrades were massacred, the Indian conflict made it unadvisable for travelers to come into Florida. Plantations were raided and burned, and massacres were not uncommon among the isolated Florida settlers. Until the Seminole Indian War was at least temporarily resolved in 1842, tourists did not come in great numbers except for a few invalids and their companions.

The consumptives, some near death, presented a melancholy scene in the town. An invalid visiting St. Augustine in 1838 commented that it was wicked to send a sick man there because of the chill northeast winds, and he noted that many had died four months before his arrival. He said that good medical attention was

available, but charges were high, about five dollars for a stranger's first visit. Another complaint was a lack of amusements and no horses or carriages for hire. However, he did praise the two hotels which accommodated forty to fifty each. The Florida House was found to be well-regulated, large, and commodious; good fires were provided. Along the sunny side of the hotel, he saw invalids cutting and whittling orange sticks for canes to take back home as presents. As for transportation, it cost five dollars to go to Jacksonville by a bad stage. A packet schooner ran regularly to Charleston, fare ten dollars, the only trouble being that sometimes it was impossible to leave the harbor for a month at a time.

An early indication of increased tourist trade, despite the threat of Indian attack, was an advertisement appearing on September 10, 1841, announcing that the City Hotel had been repaired and fitted for "Travelers, Boarders, and Invalids—rooms spacious and airy—one room 68 ft. long for Dancing, Socials and Parties."

A tourist account of 1843 showed a brighter outlook, and unlike the visitor of 1838, this one found his days busy with fishing, riding, sea-bathing, nine-pins, picnics on the islands, dances and other social activities that sometimes sent him to bed in the wee hours. So passed days, weeks, the winter. A salt water bathing house advertised its establishment as being open from sunrise until 10 P.M. The price for one visit was 12½¢; for season tickets, $5.00. Tuesdays and Thursdays were reserved exclusively for the ladies. Also during the 1840s, advertisements began appearing for local lectures and other entertainment of the kind popular in Northern cities. Then, too, daguerreotypists in the tradition of artists of old began advertising brief stays at boarding houses or hotels during the winter months to set up their cameras and equipment to capture on their silvered-plates "perfect likenesses or no charge." And in 1846 stagecoaches left three times a week for the capital city of Tallahassee!

The gloom of invalids continued into the 1850s. However, visitors in good health found many amusements, especially boating. An open rowboat, owned by six Minorcan pilots, could be hired at a reasonable charge, and elaborate picnic lunches were packed for excursions to Anastasia Island or to other local points of interest. Local people usually preferred canoes built of cypress, which held from three to twelve occupants. Visitors

View of Treasury Street, c. 1888.

"The streets of this ancient town vary in width from seven to fifteen feet, though somebody evidently blundered and laid out one twenty-five feet wide. One of the narrowest, Treasury street, contains the old Spanish Treasury building." The sign on the corner shop reads: "R.P. Sabate. Boots, Shoes, Hats."

Florida Club Headquarters, St. George Street, c. 1874. Photograph by the Florida Club.

A group of independent Boston photographers who wintered in St. Augustine had their headquarters on St. George Street. The first issue of scenes from the ancient city were custom printed by Charles Pollock, of Boston, in 1868, and were sold by subscription for the Christmas trade. For about the next ten years, the Florida Club continued to produce fine views of the area.

enjoyed watching boat pilots who stood at the beach, signaling when a vessel was expected and needed their guidance over the bar.

Another favorite amusement was riding about the countryside on ponies brought to the doors of the hotels on every nice day. One visitor said that the ponies were "larger than St. Bernard dogs, and are the most uncouth shaggy little animals extant. They are tame and docile.... They rarely have shoes, which are hardly requisite in this sandy region. Their ordinary food is coarse grass and rushes."[2]

The sportsman found the vicinity bountiful for fish and game—quails, deer, water fowl, and wild turkeys were abundant. It was said that the Florida hunter always "takes his coffee-pot with him in preference to the brandy bottle, as the climate is unfavorable to the free use of spirits. Coffee is universally drank, and it is a sufficient stimulant in this delightful country."[3]

In an advertisement of December 9, 1855, the Magnolia House (built in 1847) said that it was ready for families, invalids, and transients. The hotel faced south with forty-five rooms, and, being built of wood, it was said to be free from dampness. The restaurant featured oysters, fish, and

game. Although there was no bar room, during the era, card playing was popular and gambling was conducted at private houses with general consent. Prices at the Magnolia House in the fall of 1859 were: transient boarders, $1.25 a day; single rooms, attic, $4.50 a week; single rooms, second story, $6.50 a week; some single

The Magnolia House, March 31, 1875. Photograph by the Florida Club.

This popular hotel, built in 1847, was enlarged and improved over the years. In the mid-1870s it was completely renovated inside and out and offered single rooms and family apartments. The hotel was rebuilt in the summer of 1884 in the Queen Anne style.

Advertisement. *Guide to Florida*, 1876.

FLORIDA HOUSE,
St. AUGUSTINE.

THE Florida House, which all visitors to St. Augustine will remember, from its agreeable location and cheerful appearance—situated on St. George's Street, has undergone most important changes the past summer. A wing has been added on St. George's St., containing seventy large, well-ventilated and cheerful rooms, and the whole house has been renovated and refurnished throughout.

Guests will find the table in every way worthy of a first-class hotel, and the proprietor promises entire satisfaction to visitors.

The house will be heated throughout and gas and other conveniences furnished in every room.

I. H. REMER, Proprietor.

The Florida House, c. 1873. Photograph by E. & H.T. Anthony.

The hotel was open for guests from December to April. Extensive renovations had been done for the 1873 season. Rooms were advertised as being "large, elegantly furnished...lighted throughout with gas. A steam passenger elevator carries guests to the fourth floor. The introduction of steam into the building insures a warm and comfortable house....Electric bells in each room connect with the office. Terms, $4.00 per day." (From *Guide to Florida*, 1873.)

and double rooms with fireplaces; board exclusive of rooms, $4.00 a week. Extra meals were 37¢ and extra fires 25¢.

Once the war was over, St. Augustine entered a new era of tourism. New hotels were built, and the fashionable tourist rather than the invalid found the quaint city to his liking. All ages made the southward trek, including many women traveling in groups or young ladies escorted by their aunts, making a winter sojourn to Florida. Two ways of travel from Savannah to St. Augustine were possible in 1869. One was by steamer around the sea-coast, a run of perhaps eight hours for four dollars each way for the weekly trip. Another way was by riverboat from Jacksonville, up the St. Johns River to Picolata, at a price of two dollars for the steamer and three dollars to St. Augustine by stage. The most persistent and universal complaint in traveling to the ancient city was the dreaded eighteen mile trip from Picolata, where the St. Johns steamers let off passengers for St. Augustine. Once at the stage depot it was not unusual to wait five hours or more. Half the road was under water, and the tired, overworked horses went ahead scarcely beyond a walk. If the stage left at three, it probably reached its destination at nine in the evening, after which passengers crossed the St. Sebastian River on a rope-ferry. A rapid drive through the dark, narrow streets brought visitors to the Florida House, where often all rooms were filled. In 1869, one sportsman writing of his experiences said that no rooms were available, and he found

himself in the former "Negro quarters" in a room "innocent" of soap and water.

Apparently the commodious and comfortable Florida House of former years had gone downhill from the 1850s, because visitors complained that a comfortable hotel was lacking in the city and that a respectable boarding house with modest prices was preferable, but it was necessary to apply a week before an arrival date. The winter season was said to have commenced in early November and lasted until May.

A great delight to visitors of 1869 was the presence of a military band in the square playing national airs and other pleasant music. Also encountered in town were fashionable belles of Newport and Saratoga and clergymen from New England.

In 1870, a horse-drawn railroad, called the St. Johns Railroad, replaced the stage line, and the depot was moved two miles south of the old Picolata wharf to Tocoi.

"Old Fort, St. Augustine," c. 1887.

Bloomfield's Illustrated Historical Guide stated in 1885 that the fort occupied "about four acres of ground, and mounts one hundred guns, requiring a garrison of one thousand men.…The main entrance was by drawbridge. Over the doorway of the entrance sculptured, in a block of stone, [was] the Spanish coat of arms." An inscription with the coat of arms gave the date of the fort's completion as 1756. The fort charmed all visitors with its airy promenade, its moss-grown ancient walls built of coquina from Anastasia Island, the gloomy and mysterious recesses, the old moat, and the tales of mysterious dungeons.

The waterfront from the fort, c. 1870. Photograph by the Florida Club.

Among the objects of interest in St. Augustine was the sea wall which extended from the water battery at the fort to the barracks. Originally a Spanish structure, the wall was rebuilt in 1837 and completed in 1842 at a cost of $100,000: "In the evening, as I strolled

toward the fort to obtain a view of the imposing structure by moonlight, hundreds of visitors were seated upon the wall, listening to the music of a United States Marine band, stationed on a yacht, and witnessed a small display of fire-works from another yacht." (From a tourist's account written March 31, 1875.)

Indian prisoners, Fort Marion, 1878. Photograph by Alvord, Kellogg, & Campbell.

A new attraction at the fort in May of 1875 was a mixed group of Indians—Cheyennes, Kiowa, Comanches and Sioux—brought from Fort Sill, Oklahoma. They were quartered in an enclosure built on the ramparts and lower cells. Sometimes they entertained tourists with a war dance. A few of their squaws and children were camped on Bird Island in the harbor, making small trinkets to be sold at the fort to tourists at a good price. Captain Richard H. Pratt allowed the Indians a reasonable amount of freedom, and issued army uniforms; later some even found work in the community. They were allowed to return to the plains in April, 1878.

Sometime in the fall of 1874, "a little asthmatic tea-kettle of a steam engine…was hitched to two dilapidated boxes on wheels…the rails of pine and cypress (no iron) were worn, chipped, shivered and rotten."[4] (By 1879, the run was made in thirty-five minutes, twice a day each way, on a railway rebuilt with iron rails.) In the winter of 1874, before the steam locomotive, a distinguished party of tourists, including some Northern railroad magnates, told of a dinner at the rough hotel at the Tocoi Landing—pine boards for the table and boxes for seats: "At two o'clock the wagons came—three old street cars, each drawn by two horses or mules, tandem. In these we rushed with frantic haste, for there were too many travelers for the seats. We did not allow the old load time to get out, but piled promiscuously in.… Three horse-cars packed within and without, and a luggage van following— the crowd upon the top of the car shielded with umbrellas, toiling on over wooden rails during a three hours journey of fifteen miles, through pine forests, magnolia swamps and groves of wild oranges."[5]

Another group of travelers in the same era told of their arrival in St. Augustine from Tocoi: "[We arrived] toward sunset at the shed and bonfire which form the railroad depot of St. Augustine. This shed has never been seen open. What it contains no one knows; but it has a platform where passengers are allowed to stand before their turn comes to climb into the omnibus. The bonfire is lighted by the waiting darkies as a protection against the evening damps."[6] The omnibus brought the railway passengers across the "thicket and mud hole" out to a straight road through deep white sand, logged over with saw-palmetto. The road was built on a causeway over the San Sebastian River, and on the east side two flags and two spires could be seen of the city. On leaving the causeway, the omnibus entered the town, as one visitor said, through "a gate of foliage…forming a green arched way whose vista made beautiful the entrance to the Ancient City." Along the way, travelers passed lovely residences, one set back among the trees with an orange grove, another wide house surrounded by "piazzas overhung with ivy and honeysuckle, a garden filled with roses and every variety of flower."[7]

The driver sounded his bugle, and the omnibus came into the heart of town with its eager tourists; a group of upturned faces counted and commented upon the number of its passengers. In fact, one of the daily occupations of invalids was watching the omnibus come in. (This was also a pastime in Northern summer resorts with groups waiting on hotel verandahs for new arrivals.)

Interior view of court to barracks, February, 1896. Photograph by Jesse S. Wooley.

"There are 160 U.S. soldiers stationed. Picture shows a squad at guard-mount drill." (From Wooley's travelogue.)

The Oldest House, St. Francis Street, c. 1881.

The house on St. Francis Street, known to visitors as the "Oldest House," is documented as being the residence of a Canary Islander and his wife who lived in the house until the British occupation. The property saw many changes and renovations over the years.

Uncle Jack, the oldest person in St. Augustine, c. 1880.

"'You must see old Uncle Jack....Before the war his master sent him several times to Boston with large sums of money, and intrusted him with important business, which he never failed to execute properly. By the terms of the will he has a certain portion of the land for his lifetime. That is his old cabin....' Close down under the walls of the grand new mansion stood a low cabin, shaded by the long drooping leaves of the banana; hens and chickens walked in and out of the open door, and most of the household furniture seemed to be outside, in the comfortable Southern fashion. Uncle Jack came to meet us—a venerable old man, with white hair, whose years counted nearly a full century." (From an 1874 tourist account.)

View of St. George Street, c. 1888. Photograph by William H. Jackson.

While the men were busy with world affairs, the women liked to wander about the tiny shops in the narrow streets buying articles like brilliant flamingo wings, pink curlews, carved alligators' teeth, and coquina vases, or perhaps have a young alligator, a foot long, boxed to express north to a timid friend.

Portrait of Jack Osceola's grandson with Minorcans, at St. Augustine, February, 1891. Photograph by Miss Beck Brooks (amateur).

Some of the party wished to stay at a boarding house rather than a hotel, and one on Hospital Street was recommended—a large white mansion built of coquina, with a peaked roof and overhanging balcony. A tall black youth opened the door, and on entering, visitors found the parlor to be pleasant, decorated with gray moss and tufted grasses. The unusual feature of the house was a pet crane who lived in the yard, an immense bird standing nearly five feet high on his stilt-like legs.

Visitors explored the romantic features of the town on daily walks, stopping here and there and examining all of the points of interest. One delight was a rose tree that stood fifteen feet high with a circumference of seventeen feet, found behind an old Spanish gentleman's blacksmith shop—its annual yield more than four thousand creamy roses! And many of the roses adorned the hair of pretty young

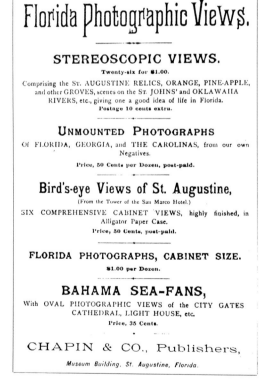

Advertisement. From *Guide to Florida*, 1873.

ladies about town. "Crowds of old ladies and gentlemen sunned themselves on the south piazzas, and troops of young people sailed and walked everywhere…with song and laughter."[8] The energetic tourists meandered through tiny shops buying palmetto hats which they immediately draped with gray moss, orangewood canes, and the inevitable cigar box containing tiny alligators to send or bring home. Also reported on the daily scene was a man with a hand organ

The new lighthouse, c. 1875.

One of the favorite sailboat rides was over to Anastasia Island to visit the new lighthouse, built in 1873: "The new lighthouse, curiously striped in black and white like a barber's pole, rose from the chaparral some distance back from the beach, one hundred and sixty feet into the clear air.…The view from the summit seemed wonderfully extensive—inland over the level pine-barrens to the west; the level blue sea to the east; north, the silver sands of the Florida main-land; and south, the stretch of Anastasia Island." (From *Harper's New Monthly Magazine*, 1874.)

View of Green Street, c. 1888.

A picturesque street not far from the convent occupied by French nuns, Sisters of St. Joseph. Note the sign: "O. Reddick Restaurant."

mask, violin, and guitar were "no longer kept up with the old taste"—the "posy dance" forgotten.[10] The wealthy visitors were building villas with orchards and gardens, reminiscent of Newport, not more than a half-hour drive to the heart of downtown. The New Englanders mingled well with those from other sections of the

St. Augustine and South Beach Railway, c. 1887.

The railway on Anastasia Island was reached by ferry from Central Wharf, near the Plaza. An 1889 advertisement noted that the rail ran from 9 A.M. until 5 P.M. on weekdays, and on Sundays every half-hour. The round trip cost twenty-five cents.

Hotel San Marco, c. 1890. Photograph by Upton and Havens.

The fashionable San Marco, built north of the City Gates, opened in 1885. A unique feature of the hotel was a pretty theatre attached to the hotel where dances and card parties were held. Tickets to these affairs cost one dollar for two and included lemonade, coffee, and cake. The hotel was destroyed by fire in 1897.

who was said to have played the same tune for two days at a time on the plaza. The large hotels were alive with activity: "The balconies of the huge St. Augustine hotel are crowded at evening when the band of the crack artillery regiment stationed there plays. In February and March the streets are gay with the costumes of the Northern cities."[9]

However, with the new influx of wealth and activity, the old romance was gradually disappearing, and it was said that the merry processions of the carnival with

country, and the city was also finding favor with the English and the French. Englishmen doffed their shooting suits to join the pleasant society gathered under the shade of orange trees, and the editorial parlors of Whitney's *Florida Press* were usually filled with men from northern and western states there to exchange opinions on current events.

Tourist accounts report that investors, mostly Northerners, expended a half-million dollars on city improvements from 1870 and that the season was so busy in late March of 1875 that no accommodations could be found at the hotels or principal boarding houses. One group of visitors in February, 1876, coming in by excursion from Fernandina on the steam propellor *Godfrey Keebler*, had made advance arrangements to stay at the St. Augustine Hotel. Although seasick on the way down, the passengers recovered on reaching land and set out to visit Fort Marion after dinner. On returning to the hotel at sunset, the party spent the evening watching the fashion display at the hotel—wealthy people from New York, Chicago, and Cincinnati displaying diamonds, rich laces, velvets, and silks, similar to the sights at Saratoga at the height of the season. Although the guests found the "Hibernian girl-waiters" not equal to the task of serving so many guests, the cuisine was good, and in the evening a fine string band played music to appreciative audiences.

Yachting had always been a favorite pastime, and in 1873 the St. Augustine Yacht Club was formally organized. A number of wealthy men and officers of the garrison built a small clubhouse out into the harbor, opposite the St. Augustine Hotel, and it became a focal point for social activities. On "illumination night" in March every yacht on the bay was lit with gaily colored lanterns, creating a picturesque evening along the waterfront.

The era of the 1880s brought great transformations to the local scene. The climate and quiet charm made it a fashionable resort competing with Jacksonville for the monied clientele. Soon,

Ponce de Leon Hotel from the Garden of the Alcazar, c. 1889. Photograph attributed to William H. Jackson.

This magnificent hotel built by the oil magnate and railroad entrepreneur Henry Morrison Flagler formally opened on January 10, 1888. A visitor of 1893 expressed her sentiments about the hotel: "…it is a melody or a poem in gray and red and green. The pearl-gray walls of shell-stone lift their cool sides between billows of foliage and masses of bright red tiling. The graceful towers, quaint dormer windows, airy loggias, and jewel-like settings of stained glass, like the palms and the fountains and galleries, all melt unnoted into the main effect." (From *Harper's New Monthly Magazine*, 1893).

Waterfront view looking toward fort, c. 1885.

The Yacht Club (to right, on water), one of the institutions of St. Augustine, had for its membership many wealthy Northerners who wintered in the city. The interior was richly furnished "in the Eastlake style" to provide every comfort for members and guests. The popular St. Augustine Hotel (left, background) accommodated 300 guests and charged four dollars per day in 1885. The building was destroyed by fire in 1887. Note the cupola of the old market in the Plaza (far left).

however, it was apparent that more luxurious hotels were needed. At least that is what Henry Morrison Flagler, the oil magnate, thought when he came to St. Augustine on his second honeymoon in December, 1883. Flagler enjoyed his winter stay, and when he visited the city again, in February of 1885, he was pleased to see the new and luxurious San Marco Hotel, constructed by the same New Englanders who had built the popular Magnolia Springs Hotel on the St. Johns River. Also, Franklin W. Smith, a Boston millionaire, had built an elaborate residence, the Villa Zorayda, a miniature reproduction of one of the palaces of the Alhambra. During the winter Flagler purchased several acres of land. Plans for a fabulous new hotel were now in the making, and when it was rumored about that the Ponce de Leon Hotel would be built, it set off a wave of land speculation. On December 1, 1885, excavation began, and although finished in May 30, 1887, the $2,500,000 hotel was not opened formally until January 10, 1888. The opening was a brilliant social event, complete with a well-known New York band to play the romantic melodies of the day in the magnificent ballroom crowded with bejeweled and richly-clad dancers.

Dining room, Ponce de Leon Hotel, c. 1888. Photograph by Upton and Haven.

"A massive yet graceful archway of red Verona marble, with spandrel patterns in variegated mosaics, leads to the great dining-hall...so bold in design and rich in decorations that, though finished in 1887, it is already famous among students of architecture." The 90′ x 150′ room provided seating for eight hundred guests.

Flagler also built the Alcazar Hotel across the way, again in the Spanish Renaissance style of architecture, the work of the same architects: "The general plan embraces an interior court with a garden and fountains surrounded by open arcades, shops, and offices, and a large restaurant. Beyond are magnificent swimming baths.... Beyond the bath are courts for tennis and croquet.... The Lodging rooms are...all provided with private baths, on what is termed in America the 'European plan.'"[11]

As news of the beautiful hotels spread about the country, the wealth and society of the nation filled the rooms. Flagler had already purchased the railway between St. Augustine and South Jacksonville, the beginning of his railroad empire in Florida, and things went so well with his hotel enterprise that in 1889 he bought the Casa Monica Hotel, adjacent to the Alcazar. He renamed it the Cordova.

Panoramic view from top of the Ponce de Leon Hotel, looking south, 1890. Photograph by Upton and Havens.

The Hotel Alcazar (above, far right) opened in late 1888, and the large hotel (above, left), formerly Casa Monica, was bought by Henry M. Flagler and renamed Hotel Cordova in 1889.

ESTABLISHED 1884.

C. F. SULZNER,

Manufacturing Jeweler,

GOLD AND SILVER NOVELTIES.

Souvenir Spoons a Specialty. ⇥⇤

(Exclusive Designs.)

Under Cordova Hotel,

Factory No. 11 St. George Street, ST. AUGUSTINE, FLA.

Advertisement. from *The Tatler*, 1896.

One of the fashionable gatherings during the season was a lawn tennis competition similar to those held in Northern resorts during the summer months. The Tropical Tournament was played on the private grounds of Villa Zorayda in March of 1888. A festive ball at the Ponce de Leon Hotel closed the event.

By 1892, the old city bustled with tourists who came to the big hotels from all over the country and from Canada and Europe. Families of high social standing met in the huge dining room of the Ponce, and many a foreign title was seen on the hotel register, as well as the names of famous American dignitaries. After the season opened, elegant shops in the Alcazar offered the latest in gowns, imported hats, jewelry, sterling ware, fine leather goods, and other luxury items. It was said by some that the season began with the Military Ball, given in the grand dining room at the Ponce de Leon Hotel, on Washington's birthday. Many heroes of the late war attended, as St. Augustine was a winter rendezvous for veterans. Also, young ladies enjoyed the attention of handsome young officers at the garrison.

Alcazar Tennis Courts, c. 1890. Photograph by Upton and Havens.

The Tropical Championship of the United States was held in St. Augustine on the second Tuesday in each March. The trophy was a massive sterling silver model of the ancient city gates. It was said that during the contest of March, 1889, more players of national reputation were gathered together than ever before. Many prominent people enjoyed the sport daily, including such well-known women as Mrs. Whitelaw Reid, Miss Hope Goddard, and Mrs. Franklin W. Smith. Special activities were also enjoyed during the tournament days—dinners, yacht races, dances, baseball, etc.

Often families rented a home in town for the season and participated in the hotel activities. Women might spend a few hours with the "social set" on the balcony of the Casino, watching the bathers in the pool below or the tennis players from the comfort of an overlooking loggia. Card-playing occupied many hours, while bits of gossip spiced the table conversations. Concerts, fairs, and hops were but a few of the affairs offered on a never-ending chain of events. On Friday evenings, "artists, in their picturesque studios in the rear of the 'Ponce' held full-dress receptions that were charming preludes to the balls that followed later."[12] The fashionable dames,

Alcazar Casino pool decorated for the annual hospital fair, 1889. Photograph by B.F. Upton.

The annual fair for the benefit of Alicia Hospital was held in mid-March under the guidance of the society matrons. Admission was twenty-five cents. Announcements proclaimed that "The visitors will enter a grotto, wander through an orange grove beside an oriental shop, visit a museum, purchase sweets…be entertained at the 5 o'clock tea, be met with a boat load of beautiful articles…visit the Alcazar table where [will be] articles made by ladies coming from every state in the Union….Near Mrs. Willoughby's boat Mrs. Henry M. Flagler will preside over a novelty sure to attract every visitor to the fair." In the tea room, souvenir spoons were sold, and a cigar stand stood near a gypsy tent.

Ride in Tally-ho coach, February, 1896. Photograph by Jesse S. Wooley.

"Here's our party starting off for a drive to north beach on Anastasia Island and to visit the black and white spiral painted lighthouse. The light flashes every three minutes and is visible for nineteen miles." (From Wooley's travelogue.)

The St. Augustine Railroad Depot, c. 1905. Photograph by Underwood & Underwood.

The depot, a two-story structure, 106' x 50', was in operation by the spring of 1888. Transportation was now made easy for the wealthy class of tourists wintering at the plush Flagler-owned hotels.

hoping to be seen, promenaded through the garden, passing by the gallery where the studios were opened.

The ballroom of the Casino was given over to children and their nurses on Saturday afternoons. Miniature balls or fancy-dress balls for the young ones, with special programs and decorations, were changed from week to week. On Saturday evenings the swimming pool at the Casino was the scene of water baseball or water polo, with high diving from the balcony railing, fancy swimming feats, and tub-races. Sundays were quiet days for church, walks or drives, and perhaps a sacred band concert at Ponce or Cordova.

When the season ended, hundreds of trunks were packed—it seemed that almost everyone left at once. In less than a week, the fair city appeared deserted. ◼

The musical quartet. February, 1896. Photograph by Jesse S. Wooley.

"The next day while wandering about the fort, I came across this quartet and wondered if they were not the ones that I heard singing the night before. They asked me to bring their pictures home with me so here they are." (From Wooley's travelogue.)

Back in the 1820s, John Randolph of Roanoke, who never lacked for an opinion, addressed Congress: "Florida, Mr. Speaker, is a land covered with water, abounding in alligators, tadpoles, serpents and all manner of noxious things; a land to which a man would not emigrate from purgatory—no sir, not even from hell itself."[1] Randolph died in 1833, of what he had called a churchyard cough, a pulmonary ailment that might have improved had he wintered in the territory he decried.

Perhaps it was such statements or writings by well-known Americans that discouraged settlement in the early days of the territory. Whatever, Florida's east coast, south of St. Augustine, remained wild and slow to develop, and it was not until after the mid-1880s, when Jacksonville and St. Augustine were booming winter resorts, that railroad crews began hammering rails southward from St. Augustine, thus opening up new resort towns along the wilderness trails traversed heretofore only by the hardiest tourists and sportsmen. Few pioneer settlers from the time of the early Spanish settlements and the Trumbull colony had survived the rigors of an unexplored land.

Transportation in the early days had been almost nonexistent. A twice-

The Halifax at Ormond, c. 1890. Photograph by O. Pierre Havens.

"The whole country about has a distinctly tropical aspect, refreshing to the eye of the traveler. There are palmettos everywhere and the 'hammocks' are now a dense mass of luxuriant verdue, where palms, magnolias, oaks, bays and myrtles are twined inextricably together by wild grapevines and Virginia creepers." (Excerpt from a letter to Hotel Ormond from a first season guest.)

HAVENS. Photo.

THE HALIFAX AT ORMOND
15

monthly mail route had been tried briefly in 1850 with passengers paying five dollars for the sea voyage aboard a schooner. During the same era, it was rumored that a good road might replace the overgrown military trail between Fort Pierce and Tampa, but the time was not yet right. Meanwhile, the government had dredged a canal connecting the Halifax with the upper Indian River, thus eliminating a difficult haulover at Mosquito Lagoon, a first step in opening up the wilderness area.

In 1882 a stagecoach route between St. Augustine and Ormond was established by a man named Buck, a character not unlike those appearing in novels about the old West, a rangy man of over six feet, who always wore high leather boots. Two other routes in the 1880s were by small schooner or steamer, from Jacksonville, or overland from the St. Johns River by a wilderness trail reminiscent of the Lewis and Clark expedition of years before—half swamp and half dry land.

The Ormond Hotel, Ormond Beach, c. 1900. Photograph by Underwood & Underwood.

"The pleasant *Ormond*… where the pleasure traveler can be comfortably lodged…fitted with all the conveniences and luxuries of the time—a hotel indeed that would do credit to any watering place." (From a letter published in the *Portland Advertiser*, April 11, 1888.) The hotel was bought by Henry Flagler in 1891 and continued on as one of the finest hotels in Florida.

The only hotel of any pretension before the 1880s was the Ocean House, in New Smyrna, where a winter visitor could look out on a muddy creek from the verandah or hunt for deer and panther in the dense forest near the house. However, it was a fertile ground for relic hunters. Many ancient earth and shell mounds awaited exploration south of the town. The only sound to break the quiet was an occasional group of noisy sportsmen heading south to Indian River country or the distant whang of axes as the "Live Oakers" chopped their way through magnificent stands of oaks, a noise destined to disappear by the 1880s.

With the arrival of the first train from St. Augustine, via Palatka, to Ormond and Daytona on December 2, 1886, a new era would begin along the east coast, heralded by shining steel tracks which would reach Miami some ten years later. The

The Florida East Coast Railroad's all-Pullman *Florida Special* alongside the fashionable Ormond Hotel, c. 1907. Photograph by Underwood & Underwood.

Train crossing the Halifax River to the Ormond Hotel, c. 1903. Photograph by Underwood & Underwood.

A special excursion train, the *Ormond*, ran between St. Augustine and Ormond Beach at the turn of the century.

special train, filled with dignitaries, was welcomed at Daytona by the Ormond brass band, a military salute by the Halifax Rifles, speeches, and a fancy banquet which featured Florida bear, Kentucky mutton, New York beef, and stuffed turkey.

The restless Florida tourist sought new sights and experiences, and the train ride to Ormond quickly became popular. From St. Augustine the journey was mostly through the pine barrens with a few orange groves to break the monotony. Suddenly, on nearing the Halifax River area, the pine barrens ended and thick masses of palmettos came into view, "guarding swampy hammocks of cypress and oak bearded with moss." The landscape changed again when the river appeared—"a wide blue arm of the sea, at whose edges the advancing forests have halted." One tourist related: "A white bridge spans the noble sheet of water, and at its farther end is seen the Ormond, whose flags and towers and galleries peep out above and between the thick foliage that forms its shady and picturesque retreat."[2]

The Hotel Ormond had opened its doors on January 7, 1888, three days before the Ponce de Leon, Flagler's fabulous hotel of St. Augustine. The Ormond would be the first of the magnificent hotels of the Florida east coast. The gala opening brought in the cream of society to dance to the strains of aristocratic music and to admire the resplendent hotel appointments which rivaled anything the famous summer resorts Cape May or Saratoga Springs had to offer. Luxuries included gas, electricity, heat, and running water—all the requirements for modern comfort. It even featured a bugle for calling guests at mealtimes! For the convenience of amateur photographers, now a fashionable pastime for tourists, a

Golfing at Ormond Beach, c. 1908. Photograph by Underwood & Underwood.

"The Golf Course at Ormond has been greatly enlarged and now has an excellent turf. Residents and tourists are admitted to membership."

The golf links at St. Augustine and Ormond, 1900.

A railroad track bisected the course at Ormond, making a hazard not found elsewhere. (From the *Florida East Coast Railway* booklet, 1900.)

darkroom was provided, a service not usually found in the plush hotels of the day.

Word about the pleasures of Ormond spread quickly to the North. The Boston *Home Journal* stated: "Ormond as a winter resort is a veritable Eden.... There are beautiful groves of orange and magnolias everywhere. Delightful shell roads stretch out in all directions. Your correspondent is not a sportsman, but if he were what a place for enjoyment! Game

127

of all kinds abounds...while in the Halifax River may be found innumerable varieties of fish."[3] Another testimonial came from the grieving widow of Henry Ward Beecher who had sought refuge at the Ormond Hotel in its first year of operation. The alleged misconduct of her deceased husband and a choir singer, some ten years before, had now been buried with the past. Mrs. Beecher wrote the proprietors: "My dear Friends: I leave the home you have managed to give to wanderers, with great regret....I cannot imagine a spot that I would sooner select for a resting place, during the remaining days or years of my life. Peaceful and lovely beyond compare...these attractions enhanced by your patience, good care and management, there is little room for criticism."[4]

After Henry Flagler bought the Ormond Hotel in the early 1890s, the town bespoke romance, becoming a rendezvous for young people, a place where courtship and respectable trysts were fashionable. Young ladies were warned that they would find life rather dull until the season opened in March. The romantic young ones were also cautioned that "In the full of the moon, boating [is] a dangerous pastime for the sentimental idly sailing on the placid waters in the witching light."[5] Also cautioned were those who strolled along the trail in the

The Florida East Coast station, New Smyrna, February, 1896. Photograph by Jesse S. Wooley.

orange-perfumed air. Young riding and coaching parties explored the strange palmetto forests or followed the river to Daytona, five miles below. It was said that the famous "Tally-ho" song roused the herons and hustled the gators as the young crews dashed merrily along on their huge tally-ho coaches.

As the century came to a close, Ormond was a New England colony who regarded Boston as the seat of learning and the hub of progress. Many of the young waitresses at the Ormond Hotel came from New England for the winter season, and they emanated an unapproachable air of respectability and education. One guest of the hotel, a staid gentleman, wrote: "The possibility that any of them were among the shadowy couples I met on the moonlit road to the sea-beach is a thought of which I was ashamed when it occurred. Those couples! What a sanctuary for cupid's victims is that white sand road to the ocean.

Bretton Inn, Ormond Beach, c. 1903. Photograph by Underwood & Underwood.

When the Bretton Inn opened in 1892, it was called Coquina Hotel. The famous ring tournaments were always held on the beach, and spectators crowded the hotel verandah to watch the event. When automobile racing became the fad after the turn of the century, a grandstand was built just north of the Inn to watch the "gasoline monsters" roar and puff their way along the beach.

Ahead of me that night I saw a swaying line of bodies, each of which appeared like one absurdly thick personage."[6]

The long stretch of smooth, hard beach running from Ormond to Daytona was not developed as a resort until the turn of the century, although in the 1890s Daytona's streets were hard and clean, having been paved with shell ground and packed into a smooth surface. Bicyclists found them perfect for their sport, which was becoming ever more popular in Florida.

However, until Daytona became an important resort, life at the Ormond on the Halifax was pleasant for tourists with boating, fishing, bowling, tennis, or golf in the morning and driving, riding, bathing, or strolling the beach in the afternoons. After dinner on cool winter evenings, guests gathered about the fireplace in the office made cozy with music, playing cards and making plans for the next day's excursion.■

View on South Beach Street, Daytona, c. 1903. The Yacht Club, founded in 1896 (above) had a membership of one hundred and nine in 1903.

The steamer *St. Augustine* in the Halifax River Canal, c. 1880.

"The Steamer starts from the pier at Ormond, and if it does not run aground too soon or too often while passing through the shallow Halifax, a delightful sail may be anticipated to Rockledge." (From *Demorest's Family Magazine*, January, 1893.)

Coquina shore line, Indian River, c. 1888. Photograph by William H. Jackson.

When the St. Johns River steamers reached Enterprise in the 1850s, a new route to Sand Point, later called Titusville, was opened. A rowboat could be hired at Enterprise for a waterland trip to Indian River, some thirty to fifty miles, depending upon the navigator's skill. In the late 1870s the route was improved when the shallow-draft steamer *Volusia*, which had a split-stern paddle wheel for quick turns, was put into service between Jacksonville and Salt Lake. From there tourists could ride the stagecoach into Titusville for an additional four dollars.

Indian River's first hotel was opened at Sand Point in the late 1860s by Colonel Henry T. Titus. His tall tales about Kansas and his hostility to fiery John Brown, the abolitionist whose body lay "mouldering in the grave," became an Indian River legend. The hotel was an attractive single story structure which had a number of rooms opening into a Spanish-style courtyard. Besides a bountiful table, hotel guests were provided with an ox-team for hauling whatever equipment tourists might bring to Salt Lake, some arduous miles inland from the river.

From a Plant System railroad booklet.

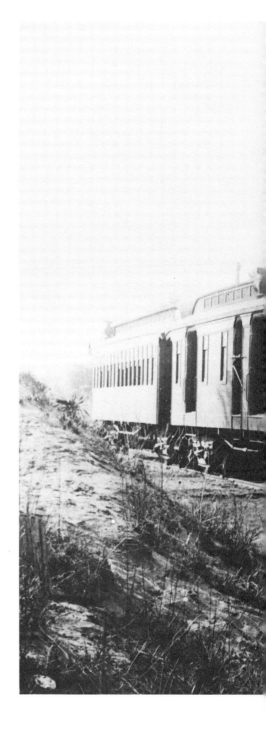

JACKSONVILLE, TAMPA & KEY WEST
RAILWAY.

WEST INDIA FAST MAIL ROUTE.

TRUNK LINE FROM JACKSONVILLE TO ALL POINTS IN SOUTH FLORIDA,

forming in connection with the South Florida Railroad, from Sanford, and its own branches and connections, absolutely the Best and Quickest Route to the following places:

ST. AUGUSTINE, PALATKA, DeLAND, TITUSVILLE, ROCKLEDGE AND ENTIRE INDIAN RIVER COUNTRY, SANFORD, TAVARES, ORLANDO, KISSIMMEE, BARTOW AND TAMPA.

SOLID TRAINS RUN FROM JACKSONVILLE TO TAMPA IN 8 HOURS carrying the Cuban Mails and Pullman Buffet Sleeping Cars, and connecting at Tampa with the magnificent Steamships "Olivette" and "Mascotte" for Key West and Havana three times a week.

ST. AUGUSTINE DIVISION—J. ST. A. & H. R. RY.

Air Line and only rail route from Jacksonville to St. Augustine. Four daily trains. Time, one hour and a half between the two cities.

Travelers from North and West arrive in Jacksonville Union Station (Savannah, Florida ank Western Railway) at which all main line trains of the Jacksonville, Tampa and Key West Railway arrive and depart, thus avoiding all vexatious transfers.

Transfer ferry boat to St. Augustine meets all trains at same station.

This road is built in the most substantial manner, and its passenger equipment is unsurpassed.

SEE THAT YOUR TICKETS READ VIA J. T. & K. W. RY.

For folders, maps of lands, of which this company owns over 2,000,000 acres, and all other information, call on or address any of the undersigned.

G. W. BENTLEY, Gen. Man.   M. R. MORAN, Gen. Supt.
ALFRED B. MASON, Land Commis'r.   L. C. DEMING, Gen. Ticket Agt.,

JACKSONVILLE, FLA.
56

Jacksonville, Tampa, and Key West Engine #4—*The Tropical Trunk Line*—stopped along the right-of-way for photographing, c. 1888. Photograph by J.A. Enseminger.

Steamer *Volusia* at dock, Jacksonville, c. 1873. Photograph by E. & H.T. Anthony.

George M. Barbour, author and Florida traveler, told about the boat in 1880: "At noon of one rainy day late in January, we took passage at Jacksonville on the old, small, odd-looking but excellent steamer *Volusia*. It is an up river steamer, an old timer, built for navigating the narrow, crooked channel of the far-up St. Johns. The steamer was crowded with passengers, including an elderly lady and her husband…and a lady residing in Jacksonville, with three small children and a nurse. The latter was on an excursion-trip, up and return; and those three children, that is to say, the two eldest boys, kept the entire party in an uneasy fidget for fear that they would or wouldn't get drowned."

One visitor coming to the area for the first time in 1876 wrote: "There is but one annoyance—insects. For real tall and lofty jumping and biting, the flea is unapproachable; but his endeavors are put to shame by mosquitos and sand-flies. The flea may be avoided.... The mosquito may be kept at bay at night, his hunting season, by a good 'bar'; but unless one is provided with an impregnable skin and a large stick of patience, he will be sure to break the commandments over sand-flies. Snakes are not numerous where the tourist need not go. This, in a word, is the good and bad of Indian River."[1]

Soon after the beginning of 1883, the little steamer *Volusia* exploded and burned while docked at Jacksonville, auspicious, perhaps, because new and large steamers were coming up the St. Johns River to Sanford. A short time later, the railroad from Sanford reached eastward to Lake Harney, not far from Titusville. Also, the first large paddle wheel steamer, suitably named *Indian River*, was put into service between Titusville and Jupiter Inlet in 1884.

The most important event for the Indian River came in 1886 with the arrival of a branch railroad line from Enterprise Junction to Titusville. It was now possible to board a train in Boston or Chicago and, with little inconvenience, travel all the way down to Jupiter Inlet.

The first booklets extolling the advantages of the Indian River were available at the Florida State Exhibition of 1888, held at Jacksonville. They proved so popular with tourists that several editions were published.

A TOURIST & HUNTER'S
GUIDE TO INDIAN RIVER
COUNTRY
1889—1890 SEASON

A winter visitor can be assured of not breathing the stifling furnace-heated atmosphere of air-tight rooms, no shrinking at the rude touch of a wintry blast, no dreaded fear of pneumonia, no doctor to feel the pulse, no long drawn-out bills for nauseating drugs, but, instead, *Nature*, free and ever-generous, will infuse new strength into the worn and tired system with a new lease on life, by giving perfect rest. Forsooth, a guest can find no pleasanter locality to pass the winter than along the Indian River. If he wishes to lead a hotel life with all the modern improvements he can do so. If he wishes to charter a sail-boat for the season, there is no section of Florida where he could get more real sport in hunting or fishing, or enjoy an out-of-door life to a greater extent.

TITUSVILLE

The town is situated near the head of navigation on the Indian River, about 16 miles south of the old canal, and is the terminus of the Jacksonville, Tampa and Key West Railway via Enterprise. Population, 1,000. Steamers connect daily with all points on the Indian River—south to Jupiter Inlet, and on alternate days north on the Halifax River as far as Daytona and Ormond. The town until the coming of the railroad, about three years ago, had something like two dozen buildings while today two hundred structures meet

A summer house along the Indian River at Rockledge, c. 1898.

the eye of the new-comer, when the iron-horse slows up at the edge of town and he gets his first view of the river.

To the west of the town there is fine rolling pine land, ideal for residences and can be had reasonably. Three firms are engaged in the shipping of fish and oysters. Among the other enterprises, the busy town has a state bank, a number of stores, with different lines, a newspaper, lumber yards, and several hotels. The Indian River and the Grand View Hotel are both $2.50 a day and $6.00 to $10.00 a week. The town also has several boarding houses, meat markets, bakeries, restaurants, barber shops, and a livery stable. Rowboats may be hired at $2.00 a day.

LA GRANGE

Situated two miles west of Titusville on the J.T. & K.W. Railway. Agriculture—Indian River oranges and vegetables.

MIMS

Situated four miles west of Titusville on the J.T. & K.W. Railway. Agriculture—oranges and lemons. The town has a comfortable hotel, a general store, post office and a neat new school. Building sites for homes have been laid out.

Pelican Island, Indian River, c. 1888. Photograph by William H. Jackson.

Called the greatest curiosity of the region, Pelican Island was often known as the Rookery or the Pelicanry. A refuge for tens of thousands of pelicans, it was just above the Halifax Canal on the steamer route to Titusville. For centuries the birds had built their nests in a forest of dead trees. The stems and branches stood bare and gaunt, crusted white against the dark beyond.

Duck hunting, Rockledge, 1896. Photograph by Jesse S. Wooley.

"If you are fond of duck hunting you should visit the Indian River at Rockledge, this is 'Huntsman's Paradise.' The river is swimming at all times of the day with ducks—Ducks innumerable. These two gentlemen caught 47 in two hours—How's that for duck shooting!" (A comment from Wooley's travelogue.)

AURANTIA

On the west bank of Indian River, opposite the new coast canal. Nothing of importance here except the tidy depot of the J.T. & K.W. Railway. Town lots free to those who will build a neat house or store, and a large lot will be given for a hotel or boarding house.

HAULOVER

This post office is located on an isthmus separating the Indian River from Mosquito Lagoon, about nine miles northeast of Titusville. The Atlantic Coast Canal Company is currently working on a canal 3,350 feet long to replace the old canal which is growing more narrow each year.

HEATH

Directly east of Titusville on the north bank of the Banana Creek. This section, being between the Indian River and the Atlantic Ocean, is almost entirely free from frosts. Fish and game can be found here in abundance. Wild ducks use the region as a feeding ground and congregate here by the thousands. An attractive area for the sportsman.

COMMENTS AND PHOTOGRAPHIC EXCERPTS ABOUT THE INDIAN RIVER FROM THE JESSE S. WOOLEY STEREOPTICON TRAVELOGUE OF FEBRUARY, 1896

CANAVERAL

A large parcel of land lying between the Banana River and the Atlantic Ocean. Noted for its citrus trees. The river teems with fish the year around, yet land is comparatively cheap. Canaveral lighthouse is one of the finest on the Atlantic coast having a revolving flash light and stands 139 feet tall. The post office is about five miles west of the light.

HARDEEVILLE

First mail and steamboat landing, ten miles south of Titusville. An eligible site is offered free to anyone who will build a good hotel thereon.

COURTNEY

Twelve miles southeast of Titusville on Merritt's Island. Has a daily mail service, north and south. Agriculture—Indian River oranges, pineapples, bananas, guavas. Excellent soft water from driven wells. A fine location with a view of the bay. Needs a store, hotel or boarding house.

CITY POINT

About sixteen miles south of Titusville. Has a regular steamboat landing, daily mails, a telegraph and express office, and a good general store. There is no hotel but a fine boarding house where guests will find good cheer and comfortable quarters. Has an excellent day school, a Sunday school, and preaching every Sunday.

Ferry to Honeymoon Lake, Merritt Island, February, 1896. Photograph by Jesse S. Wooley.

"We hailed the ferry man from the opposite shore who came over and rowed us back in an immense rowboat. There were 13 in the boat but had no ill luck." (A comment from Wooley's travelogue.)

An Indian River steamer off Rockledge, February, 1896. Photograph by Jesse S. Wooley.

Mr. Wooley and party saw this steamer from their hired launch *Plaza* as they traveled downriver.

Miss Kate's Novelty and Tackle Store, Rockledge, c. 1906. Photograph by Underwood & Underwood.

MERRITT

East shore of Indian River, nearly opposite City Point. The town has some handsome residences and a Baptist Church presenting an attractive sight when viewed from a passing steamer. A fine hotel has been erected near the landing and visitors can also find good accommodations at several private boarding houses. In season, Cleveland Jelly Factory has daily shipments of guava jelly to all northern points.

COCOA

Located nineteen miles south of Titusville on west bank. The ground gently slopes up from the river to about forty feet and affords a beautiful view from the height. A large business section has four merchandise stores, a lumber yard, a news dealer, drug store, dentist, jeweler, barber, two shoemakers, a blacksmith, a billiard saloon, a soda-water stand, a meat market, a weekly newspaper, a restaurant, two hotels and a dressmaking shop. Sunday schools and four churches, white and colored, open every Sunday for services. The Oleander Point Regatta Association holds yacht races each season.

ROCK LEDGE

About a mile south of Cocoa. The post office was established in 1876, and the town was incorporated in March of 1887. The fashionable tourist has come here in great numbers for the past few years preferring the milder winters here to those of Ormond and St. Augustine. A beautiful paved walkway is being extended the whole length of the settlement, winding along the many curves of the river bank, beneath the shade of live-oaks and palmettos. The town has three large hotels—Indian River at $4.00 a day; New Rockledge, $2.50 a day; and the Tropical House, $3.00 a day. Also, several large boarding houses and two restaurants can entertain all who come and will suit both taste and purse. Rowboats may be hired at $2.50 a day and sail-boats at $4.00 a day. Northern visitors have built a number of houses for their winter quarters. President Cleveland stopped here on his Indian River trip last year (1888).

The Promenade (Indian River Boulevard), Rockledge, c. 1903. Photograph by Underwood & Underwood.

The hotel launch *Plaza*, 1896. Photograph by Jesse S. Wooley.

"Accordingly we chartered the naptha launch *Plaza* and started off early in the morning for Merritt Island and 'Fairy Land.'" (A comment from Wooley's travelogue.)

GEORGIANA

On the Indian River side of Merritt's Island, twenty-five miles south of Titusville. The town has a grocery and hardware store, post office, tin shop, and ten or twelve dwellings. Sunday school and church services are offered by the Methodist Episcopal Church. Fish and game are abundant. Reasonable rates and good board are available with private families, and, if desired, quiet restful home life. About a mile south of the village is "Fairy Land," one of the most picturesque places on the river.

EAU GALLIE

About forty miles south of Titusville, and has one of the best harbors for sailing crafts of all descriptions. The shores are high and rocky, and the water clear and deep. The settlement has a store, church, school, and a three-story hotel with accommodations for fifty or more guests. It has daily mail and telegraphic communication with the outside world.

MELBOURNE

About three miles south of Eau Gallie on the west side of the river. Crane Creek, coming in from the west, forms a bay which makes an excellent harbor for sail or rowboats. An effort has been made to make the town an attractive winter resort. It has two general stores, a newspaper, meat market, two lumber yards, three hotels and a telegraph office. The town has daily mail from the North and is the terminus for tri-weekly mail from south Florida. A steam ferryboat crosses the river to the east side where a wharf and tramway to the beach is under construction. One or two hotels are being built to take advantage of the delightful winter climate and surf bathing every month of the year.

The freeze of February 8, 1890, Melbourne. Photograph by S. Shear, the Indian River photographer.

A Coach Whip snake, February, 1896. Photograph by Jesse S. Wooley.

"He was a very sociable old gent especially with the ladies who got on the right side of him with a box of bon-bons. It seemed to touch the right spot, and he opened his heart, and invited us to his strawberry patch and told us to help ourselves." (A comment from Wooley's travelogue.)

Florida East Coast Train at Fort Pierce Station, February, 1896. Photograph by Jesse S. Wooley.

"At Fort Pierce station 'Billy Bow-Legs' a Seminole Indian from Lake Okeechobee put in his appearance. Settlement of 160 Seminole Indians in Everglades—Billy is their chief." (A comment from Wooley's travelogue.)

Indian River orange grove, February, 1896. Photograph by Jesse S. Wooley.

"Upon reaching the shore we ascended a small hill—the sight that met our gaze made our mouths water but our appetite was somewhat repressed when we noticed a sign on a tree that read as follows—'Visitors are requested not to handle fruit or flowers. Indian River oranges 80¢ to $1.00 per doz.' The proprietor was very careful that no branches should be broken off but at the sight of a crisp $1.00 bill he was persuaded to allow my friend to break off 2 branches each with 3 oranges on." (A comment from Wooley's travelogue.)

ST. LUCIE

One of the oldest settlements, nearly opposite the Indian River Inlet, and about fifty miles south of Melbourne. Site of Fort Capron during the Indian War years, although nothing now remains. The river at this point has extensive oyster beds and turtle and other fishing is excellent. Tarpon fishing is featured with all the prestige due the hero who succeeds in landing one of the monster beauties. Tourists or sportsmen will find accommodations at good boarding houses. A large fine general store can be found at Fort Pierce about four miles down river.

EDEN

About eleven miles south of Fort Pierce on the west side of Indian River. The town is on an imposing high bluff which runs many miles southward along the river. Extensive fields of pineapples were uninjured in the great freeze of 1886. Here comfortable lodgings can be found by the pleasure-seeker or invalid. An attempt has been made to restore the lost "garden of Eden" where the owner claims to have found the "fountain of Youth."

147

Boating in the Jupiter Narrows, c. 1888. Photograph by William H. Jackson.

One of the 1890 guide books told about Jupiter Narrows: "Here the mangrove assumes its subtropical vigor, and it may afford amusement to athletes to penetrate a mangrove swamp by...climbing from root to root."

JUPITER INLET

The inlet is about 154 miles south of Titusville, and is the southern terminal point of a long series of rivers that skirt the east coast of Florida in an almost unbroken chain. The steamer *S.V. White* leaves Melbourne on Tuesday, Thursday, and Saturday at 4:00 A.M. arriving at Jupiter at 7:00 P.M. the same day. On alternate days the steamer leaves Jupiter at 4:00 A.M. arriving at Melbourne at 7:00 P.M. The connecting steamer *Rockledge* leaves Melbourne daily for Titusville at 8:10 P.M. The Jupiter and Lake Worth Railroad has replaced the stage line and now runs south to Palm Beach from the Inlet. Along the inlet it is sparsely settled, the main buildings being the lighthouse, the signal station, and the keeper's houses. A large riverboat, the *Chattahoochee*, has been moored to a wharf and is now a floating hotel, $3.00 a day. The hotel has a naptha launch, and rowboats are for hire at reasonable rates. There is no better fishing than found at Jupiter Inlet. Bluefish, bass, pompano, runners, ladyfish, sheepshead, and other varieties can be taken with a rod. Sharks abound at the inlet and may be caught with suitable tackle. Panthers and wildcats still prowl about the settlement at night. It is interesting to stand on the upper deck of the *Chattahoochee* and watch the revolving rays of the lighthouse as they touch different points of sea and shore. For the naturalist, the beach on either side of the inlet is strewn with sun-cured sponges, sea-beans, cocoanuts, and a hundred strange forms of animal and vegetable life swept up from the coral reefs by the Gulf Stream.

The Jupiter Lighthouse, c. 1866. Watercolor. Sketched by Alfred R. Waud.

"No one capable of mounting the stairs should fail to cross over to the lighthouse and enjoy the impressive view that spreads map-like to the horizon in all directions. From the lantern gallery one may see, in clear weather, more than forty miles up and down the coast, and across the intervening forest nearby to the shores of Lake Okeechobee." (From a Florida guide book.)

The Anchorage at Jupiter Inlet, c. 1890.

The very popular Vaill's floating hotel, the *Chattahoochee* (above, far right), "is moored about a mile from the inlet, and nearly opposite the mouth of Jupiter Sound. From the upper deck there is a good view of the inlet and the neighboring waters."

Children at play. Jupiter Inlet, c. 1890.

The steamer *Santa Lucia* unloading passengers, Jupiter Inlet, c. 1890.

After the railroad reached West Palm Beach, steamer service on the river was discontinued, and the *Santa Lucia* became Flagler's work ship at Miami.

The yacht *Zianetta New York*, Rockledge waterfront, c. 1905. Photograph by Underwood & Underwood.

A series of events quickened the pace for bringing in settlers and tourists. Flagler had bought his first railroad in 1886, which ran from Jacksonville to Palatka, via St. Augustine. He added an important link to his empire in 1888, when he joined his rail line from Jacksonville-Palatka with the new road to Daytona—the name now changed to the Jacksonville, St. Augustine and Halifax River Railway. In November of 1892, he pushed an extension south to New Smyrna. The die had been cast, and again the steel rails moved southward. On February 6, the regular daily train #27 reached Rockledge. To make the trip

The Florida East Coast Railway Station, Rockledge, February, 1896. Photograph by Jesse S. Wooley.

memorable, passengers were told: "At Shiloh, 105 miles south of St. Augustine, the first view of the Indian River [can] be had from the left side of the train." Once again the name changed; it was now the Jacksonville, St. Augustine and Indian River Railway—*East Coast Line*. The line advertised that it would reach Palm Beach on November 1, 1893, an ambitious promise which could not be fulfilled. However, rail construction kept more or less to a timetable—train #27 reached Eau Gallie on June 26, 1893. Other towns quickly followed—Melbourne (#27) on October 2; Sebastian (#23), December 11; and on January 29, 1894, Fort Pierce (#23) was reached. At each temporary terminal point along the river, the railroad had connecting steamers for the balance of the trip to Jupiter Inlet, where the Celestial Railroad ran about eight miles south into Palm Beach.

East Coast Line.
The St. Augustine Route

The Jacksonville,
St. Augustine & Indian River R'y

IS UNDER CONTRACT FOR COMPLETION
TO LAKE WORTH

NOVEMBER 1, 1893.

The Company has large bodies of timber and farming lands along the line of its railroad, which it offers to settlers upon easy terms and at reasonable prices;

IN FACT,

Every Inducement is held out to
ACTUAL SETTLERS.

J. R. PARROTT,
VICE-PRESIDENT.

W. L. CRAWFORD,
GENERAL SUPERINTENDENT.

JOSEPH RICHARDSON,
GENERAL PASSENGER AGENT.

GENERAL OFFICES: - - ST. AUGUSTINE, FLORIDA.

From a railroad brochure, 1893.

The Plaza Hotel from the Indian River, Rockledge, c. 1900. Photograph by Underwood & Underwood.

One of the hotel's visitors related: "We are very pleasantly located at the *Plaza*. A fine new hotel kept by a man whose whole aim seems to be the entertainment of his guests."

Had Mr. Flagler stopped his railroad at this point or had he built one of his fabulous hotels along the Indian River, the history of the area might have been quite different. However, Rockledge did have a brief period, from about 1890 to 1895, when polite society bestowed upon the town its monied patronage. One member of the elite wrote about the resort in 1893: "This is the first and only landing that rivals Ormond in fashionable society." ■

12

Life in the tropics. Palm Beach, February, 1896. Photograph by Jesse S. Wooley.

"With here and there a palmetto thatched "shack" in which one may pass a winter very comfortably." (Comment from Wooley's travelogue.) It was said that the first pioneers of Palm Beach lived in palmetto shacks when they settled the area in the mid-1870s.

When the Florida East Coast train— #23, leaving Jacksonville, 8:50 A.M., arriving West Palm Beach, 9:30 P.M.—Flagler's first daily train, crossed over the Jupiter Creek trestle on the evening of April 2, 1894, an important cycle of events in Florida's history began. Those events led to a resort story unrivaled elsewhere.

The United States Coast and Geodetic Survey, in its 1887 chart, indicated the future Palm Beach as "The Lake Worth Settlement." The village, a narrow strip of land along the ocean, fronting on Lake Worth, was named in memory of General William J. Worth of Seminole Indian War fame.

Who gave Palm Beach its pretty name? Three pioneers, who met in the rear of a local store in 1887 chose the name Palm City, from which came Palm Beach. A Spanish barque reportedly came ashore in the late 1870s scattering some twenty thousand cocoanuts: "Many thousands of nuts were gathered and planted…in circles, singly, and in groups, with the results that now the cocoa palm lifts its graceful fronds above every roof, lines walks and avenues, and lends a tropical aspect to the whole settlement."[1]

In 1885 the village showed little resemblance to the fabulous resort to come. The colony had two general stores,

"Before Sunrise on Lake Worth," view taken from **West Palm Beach, c. 1898.**

a scattering of local pioneers, and little else until the following year when Northern visitors crowded Dimick's Cocoanut Grove House, the only hotel, from January to April. Before the season was over, a gentleman from far-off Denver, Colorado, bought a forty-acre homestead for $10,000 (a considerable sum for early Palm Beach) with the intention of building a mansion before the next season. Later, he reaped a tidy profit when Flagler paid him $75,000 for the Royal Poinciana Hotel site.

Transportation before the 1889-90 season had been difficult, as Jupiter Inlet was the end of the line for Indian River steamers. A rough stage ran from the inlet to Palm Beach over a heavy road where horses rarely moved faster than a walk. Passengers and freight were put into a three-spring, three-seated wagon, drawn by two mules for a fare of two dollars, with an extra dollar for trunks. The riders were let off on the west side of the lake

and ferried across to Palm Beach.

The Jupiter and Lake Worth Railway was completed in time for the 1889-90 season; it was known as the Celestial Railroad because of its four stations, Jupiter, Venus, Mars, and Juno. The eight-mile track ran from Jupiter Inlet to the head of Lake Worth, where two small steamers paddled another eight miles to Palm Beach.

By 1890, the town's character began to emerge. Tasteful cottages and a few costly mansions lined the lake. Norton's handbook for 1890 extolled the pleasures to be found at Palm Beach: "A smooth walk, shaded and for the most part well kept, tempts to extended excursions, and leads at intervals through private grounds that are marvels of beauty. Oleanders and poincianas here are trees twenty or thirty feet high, and gigantic cacti stand like sentinels on the lawns; the hibiscus, red, white and yellow, lavishes its blossoms in every garden. From every house a walk or trail leads across the peninsula to the

A Gem of Lake Worth, Palm Beach, 1890. Photograph by O. Pierre Havens.

"A natural sea-wall is formed along the shore by underlying coralline rock, and some of the more wealthy residents, not satisfied with this, have added an artificial wall." (From Norton's handbook, 1890.)

The Ramble, Palm Beach, 1892. Photograph by O. Pierre Havens.

ocean beach...laden with shells and marine curiosities that tempt collectors to wander for miles along the sands...and looking out to sea rarely a day passes that several south-bound steamers are not seen close in to avoid the current that rushes northward at four to fives miles an hour, while further out in the Gulf Stream north-bound vessels are speeding in the opposite direction."

Palm Beach was rather peaceful for a few years despite the improvement in transportation. Each season brought new faces, many from the roster of the nation's most important people, many of whom began building winter homes. The tran- quility ended in March of 1893, when it was whispered that Flagler, the legendary promoter, the investor in large hotels and railroads, was going to build a huge hotel in Palm Beach. His agent had come down from St. Augustine to buy the hotel site, and if the present rumor was correct, had just paid $30,000 for a tract of land west of the lake, where Flagler proposed plat- ting a new town to be called West Palm Beach. Land speculation came overnight. Prices jumped from $150 to $1,000 an acre and upward, a veritable gold rush. Many local residents suddenly found themselves rich by selling and reselling. The heavy buyers were from out-of-

The beach, Palm Beach, February, 1896. Photograph by Jesse S. Wooley.

"We also visited Cragin's cactus garden on Lake Worth. 300 varieties, also a travelers tree. From here we walked across the narrow strip of land and came back by the sea. Have you discovered our foot prints in the sand? We are now over 1500 miles from New York and at the end of the railroad in Southern Florida." (Comment from Wooley's travelogue.)

town—Chicago, New York, Philadelphia, and other cities, even some from England.

Preparations for the new Royal Poinciana Hotel moved at a fast pace. Men and materials began pouring into Palm Beach, and shacks, tents, and boarding houses went up in a section called "The Stix" near the hotel site. About one thousand men, mostly master craftsmen, were brought in and work began on May 1. Transportation for the tremendous amounts of materials needed for construction was the most serious problem, because everything had to be shipped from where the railroad ended at Eau

Gallie on to Jupiter by Indian River steamer, by rail to Juno, and again by boat to Palm Beach. Every available craft was put into service, and a small army of men was kept at each changing point. They worked night and day seven days a week. The freight bill on the Celestial Railroad alone came to $60,000.

The locals referred to the new hotel as the largest in the world, an overstatement as there were larger ones in Northern resorts. However, the Royal Poinciana was very large with 540 bedrooms, a dining room that seated one thousand guests, public rooms, parlors, a rotunda, wide

The Ramble, Lake Worth, 1890. Photograph by O. Pierre Havens.

Many new varieties of tropical vegetation were planted in Palm Beach around 1890: "One of the most attractive sights on the shore of the lake is the garden of Charles Cragin which contains a collection of over 500 varieties of cacti." (C.V. Hine, 1891.)

porches, innumerable hallways, and basement rooms with every convenience and comfort.

The hotel opened on February 11, 1894, with little fanfare and less than twenty guests, but well ahead of schedule. Soon an enthusiastic and incredibly wealthy clientele filled it. Within a few years, two additions doubled its size.

Meanwhile, the town of West Palm Beach became a reality. Flagler paved the streets with shell and sold a number of

area was part of Dade at that time) reprinted news items from July, 1894. The following items were selected at random from the booklet about West Palm Beach and the area:

IMPORTANT EVENTS

As Compiled from the Columns of The *Gazetteer* from July 4th, 1894 to Time the Paper was Burned Out.

July 11, 1894. Enlargement and improve-

"The Styx," Palm Beach, 1894.

Shacks, tents, and boarding houses were put up in a hurry and rented at high prices. The housing sheltered the one-thousand-strong work crew who built the Royal Poinciana Hotel in 1893. When the hotel was completed, the Styx was demolished.

lots for stores and homes. By the time the first Florida East Coast train rolled into town, a station had been built, and the community bustled with an air of municipal vitality.

Because Palm Beach was in a "dry" county, the hotel could not serve alcohol. The local people, however, said there was no shortage of whiskey if you knew the right people. In the fall of 1894, the question was put to ballot—the "wets" won, and the hotel could satisfy yet another of its customers' desires.

In 1896, the *History and Guide of Dade County, Florida* (the Palm Beach

ments on the Royal Poinciana about completed.

July 25, 1894. The Y has grown to ten business establishments.

July 28, 1894. Wildcat attacks little daughter of W.E. Sears. City hall and prison commenced (crime had sharply increased, 17 murders since the Poinciana started).

August 4, 1894. Robert Ganzberg, a barber, accidentally shot in front of the Seminole Hotel last Thursday morning, dying soon after.

August 15, 1894. Registration shows over 100 voters in town. The city jail gets its

"Where the water lilies bloom in March, West Palm Beach, Florida," 1895. (From Wooley's travelogue.)

The second *Bethesda by the Sea* church, Palm Beach, February, 1896. Photograph by Jesse S. Wooley.

"A pretty church whose pastor is very fortunate, in winter has this charge and in summer one on St. Huberts Island, Raquette Lake." (Comment from Wooley's travelogue.)

first lodger—a Bohemian. John H. Williams shot another colored man over a game of 'skin,' severely wounding him. Excursion to St. Augustine last week carried a large crowd.

September 5, 1894. C.I. Cragin awards the contract for a new bath house on the beach. Shelling of streets completed.

September 10, 1894. Indian mounds near middle river examined and many relics of a pre-historic race found. *Gazetteer* threatened with libel suit.

October 3, 1894. The name West Palm Beach discovered to have 13 letters; so far has had three storms and three fires. Monday came the predicted storm, lasting the better part of two days and doing considerable damage to wharf and boats.

October 13, 1894. Canal between New and Hillsboro rivers completed.

County officers elected.

November 10, 1894. The election passed off quietly on the 5th for town officers. For incorporation, 74; against, 1. Mr. Tyndall of Jupiter bitten on the leg by a rattlesnake.

December 12, 1894. Mr. Flagler, Plant, and a number of railroad magnates arrived on the 3rd. Water works completed. New York papers reach us in 40 hours.

January 2, 1895. On the first day of January, 1894, only one house stood in West Palm Beach. The newly built ferry boat

was put in commission Sunday morning.

January 12, 1895. The effects of the cold wave on Dec. 28 were not as bad as first thought. Fisherman caught a 25 pound pompano. Lettie Dickson, who murdered Josephine Johnson Christmas night, was caught in men's attire just as she was boarding a schooner at Biscayne Bay.

January 26, 1895. Seminole Hotel bar robbed of $250.00.

February 14, 1895. Thermometer 24° at Melbourne, 38° here. The Palm Beach Yacht Club will give a regatta on the 22nd.

February 28, 1895. New Wharf being built [at] north end of Flagler property. J.D. Crimmins, of New York, catches a jew fish from the surf with hook and line weighing 355 pounds. Mrs. Grant [President Grant's widow] visits the lake.

March 21, 1895. Miss Deborah Woolley, chambermaid at the Royal Poinciana, fell down the freight elevator from the third story to the basement Friday morning, killing her instantly. Ex. Gov. Flower and family, of New York, visit the lake.

April 1, 1895. The *Gazetteer* begins a crusade against crime that ends in breaking up one of the leading dens.

April 11, 1895. The bodies have been removed from old to new cemetery.

April 18, 1895. Mr. Flagler decides on building the Palm Beach Inn; also a large clubhouse. Masked ball given in aid of County Exposition Fund.

May 4, 1895. The Indian River Steamboat Co. decides to lay their steamers up. The last of the hotel help gone; a most prosperous season.

May 18, 1895. Turtle season and egg hunting in vogue. Colored band gives an excursion to Lantana. Threats to hickory whip editor of *Gazetteer* by a county official.

May 25, 1895. Eight buildings nearing completion ranging in cost from $1,000 to $3,500. Editor of *Gazetteer* arrested on a warrant for criminal libel sworn out by the sheriff.

June 8, 1895. Engineers begin the survey for extension of East Coast Railway to Miami. John Seabold, baker from Palatka, establishes bakery.

June 15, 1895. Electrician A.T. Best, of the Flagler hotels, arrives with force to put plant in Royal Poinciana and Palm Beach Inn. Grading on the East Coast Railroad extension begins. First carload of keg beer arrives.

July 4, 1895. Celebration succeeds.

August 10, 1895. Str. *Hattie* begins regular service between here and New River.

September 25, 1895. Track laying on East Coast Railway extension commenced. Work commenced on Lake Worth rail-

The wharf, West Palm Beach, March 27, 1895. Photograph attributed to Fred Hand.

"Lake Worth, the fisherman['s] paradise. You would doubt my big fish stories if I didn't show you the real facts. 128 King fish, 15 lb. each, caught with 3 lines in one day. They say fish are so thick in Lake Worth that they rub their scales off." (Comment from Wooley's travelogue.) Wooley missed the local gossip about winter visitors: "Nearly everyone had a boat and during the season it became a pleasure fleet for sailing tourists, but Mr. Tourist paid for everything he touched and a good round price, too."

Advertisement from *History and Guide of Dade County, Florida*, 1896.

"His gallery is fitted up for any class of work, and he has the well earned reputation of being one of the best artists in the country."

road bridge last week. Contract let to Capt. Ross for ocean pier in front of Palm Beach Inn.

October 19, 1895. Announcement of the establishment of the Palm Beach-Nassau S.S. Line. J.T. Flood awarded contract for erection of "help quarters" for the Inn.

November 23, 1895. News received that Samuel Barton, a winter resident, died at his home in New York. Work on ocean pier to begin at once. Bridge gang go south to put up railroad bridges.

December 7, 1895. The grand jury refuses to consider the sheriff's charge of libel against the editor of the *Gazetteer*. Corry's museum building at Palm Beach completed.

January 4, 1896. Fire broke out in the Midway Plaisance saloon and restaurant about 2 P.M. Thursday. Entire square fronting on Banyon Street burned. Both electric light plants for the Flagler hotels, the largest in the country, completed.

January 25, 1896. Buildings are going up rapidly on burnt district; all will be replaced. On the 18th the ladies of West Palm Beach gave a leap year's ball.

February 20, 1896. Fire broke out about ten o'clock on Clematis Avenue and soon all the south side of the square was in ashes. One of the town's newspapers, several large stores, and a number of professional offices entirely destroyed.

Postscript: Due to the disastrous fire of Feb. 20, 1896 the *Guide's* account of events abruptly ends.

By the fall of 1896, Palm Beach residents sent word north that, while the summer had been hotter and longer than usual, a number of interesting events had occurred. It was pointed out that no one had died of heat prostration, whereas the heat waves in Northern cities had resulted in a hundred or more deaths. One story reaching the North appealed to the imagination—a fight to the death between an alligator and a shark, both very large; the shark was badly cut up, with great pieces bitten out of him, while the alligator had lost a foreleg close to his body. Also of interest was the news that a ten-foot crocodile had been captured, killed, and mounted, and put on view in Professor Corry's Palm Beach museum. Another bit of gossip drifting north was about the owner of a local hotel, who had fallen asleep in a hammock after placing his pipe on the ground. When he awoke, the pipe was gone, but later in the summer he found it minus the stem. A hermit crab was using it as a shell.

For the winter season of 1896-97, the Four Hundred introduced many of the summer pleasures enjoyed at Newport, Bar Harbor, and Saratoga. Life in Palm Beach centered more and more around the fashionable Royal Poinciana and the newly opened Palm Beach Inn. Dress for the gentlemen and their ladies was no longer *dishabille*—ceremony and etiquette were now the vogue. Other similarities to the elite summer resorts were cottages being built near the hotels, reminiscent of the prestigious villas at Newport. The elite yachting crowd also moved their headquarters south to Palm Beach for the winter. A winter home in Palm Beach was now as fashionable as a

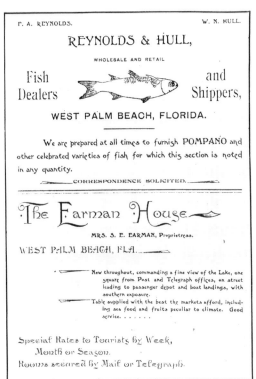

Advertisement from *History and Guide of Dade County, Florida*, 1896.

summer residence in Bar Harbor, Campobello, or Tuxedo Park.

Health had always been a serious consideration for the wealthy, and in bygone years society had favored the "waters" at Saratoga. Wintering in Palm Beach now insured longevity with its many outdoor pastimes, including pleasant hours on the

Royal Poinciana Hotel, Palm Beach, February, 1896. Photograph by Jesse S. Wooley.

"Five dollars per day and up. Mostly up—*Hold up your hands*—cocoanut trees here in abundance." (Comment from Wooley's travelogue.)

golf course.

The smart young set developed their own customs at the notable resorts. One favorite pastime was "hotel hopping" from one fashionable watering spa to the next. When the Florida season opened, the game began at the "Ponce" in St. Augustine, with a yoo-hoo and a wave, then on to Ormond, Orlando, Tampa, and finally Palm Beach, with side trips to Miami and Nassau.

In 1898, Flagler brought gambling to Palm Beach—a cherished amusement for polite society at the better resorts. Morrissey's in Saratoga, considered the best house in the country for high stakes, would take second place to the proposed gambling palace. Flagler's Beach Club was a quiet operation because gambling was illegal in Florida. The club featured an epicurean restaurant, and membership was by invitation only. Edward R. Bradley, from the plush Bacchus Club of St. Augustine, came south to manage the new club. He knew all the right people, was dignified, discreet, and had the talents needed for a smooth operation. Eventually, the casino was as well known as the one in Newport.

Palm Beach also received the kind of quiet publicity the wealthy always enjoyed. Joseph Jefferson, the famous and

Overlooking Lake Worth and West Palm Beach from the Royal Poinciana Hotel, February, 1896. Photograph by Jesse S. Wooley.

The railroad and footbridge (toll five cents) connecting Palm Beach with the mainland were almost completed when this photograph was taken.

The Royal Poinciana from the lake dock, February, 1896. Photograph by Jesse S. Wooley.

"The Station," Palm Beach Inn, February, 1896. Photograph by Jesse S. Wooley.

"Custom House officers looking through baggage bound for Nassau, Palm Beach Inn." (Comment from Wooley's travelogue.) Steamship service was inaugurated between Palm Beach and Nassau on January 15, 1896, on every Tuesday, Thursday, and Saturday thereafter. Meals and berth for round trip came to thirty dollars.

respected actor of the American theatre, wintered in Palm Beach. The actor's portrayal of Rip Van Winkle had gained him international fame and admiration. Jefferson was also a close fishing companion of President Cleveland. While in Palm Beach, he lived in his oceanfront home "The Reefe." The *Munsey Magazine* reported in 1902: "Almost any morning the famous old actor may be found bundled in shawls sprawling on the sands,

and usually surrounded by a company of children. Bright days he spends on the lake fishing and usually getting a full basket."[2]

When the century closed, Palm Beach was a focal point for high society newspaper reportage with stories of afternoon teas, dinners, concerts, and balls in a setting of fantasy, grace, and beauty—a land of enchantment. ▮

Bathing scene, Palm Beach, 1903.

Saltwater swimming pool. The Casino, Palm Beach, 1896. Photograph by Jesse S. Wooley.

On February 5, 1896, the temperature of the pool was 76°, temperature of the surf 73°: "Warm sea water baths on an elaborate scale are provided for those enervated scions of wealthy sires who cannot endure the chill buffeting of the surf." For the guests who liked to gossip from a porch rocker, it was whispered: "There is a great swimming tank, wherein a titled lady is said to have disported herself in a man's bathing attire, to the amazement of the onlookers."

Ocean front, Palm Beach, 1905.

Expert lifeguards, often coming from the swank Northern seaside resorts, watched over the casino's guests during swimming hours.

An early Palm Beach home, 1890. Photograph by O. Pierre Havens.

By the turn of the century, Palm Beach became the millionaire's playground with its restful retreats and cocoanut shaded walkways.

"Harvesting the Cocoanuts," 1891. Photograph by George Barker.

A number of Northerners came to south Florida late in the century with the idea that a cocoanut plantation would make them rich. About the only profit came from tourists, who often mailed the fruit home.

At the close of the Civil War, Judah P. Benjamin, former Confederate Secretary of State, while fleeing from the wrath of the Yankee avengers, put into Biscayne Bay for water and provisions. He spoke of the great beauty he found and predicted a bright future for the area. He also remarked that the present inhabitants were a hard-looking set of beachcombers and deserters, along with an assortment of cutthroats. A few years later, visitors to the bay wrote that the cutthroats had disappeared without a trace.

In 1875, a touring English sportsman stopped by Miami for a brief visit, anchoring his schooner near the mouth of the Miami River, not far from Brickell's new trading store. Innumerable English travelers toured America in the 1870s, and each, it seemed, recorded opinionated

views on what they saw. The boat's anchor had hardly dropped before this visitor found fault with the area. Insects alone, he declared, were enough to make the region uninhabitable for the majority of men. Two species he found to be particularly objectionable: "a large horse-fly, about five times the common size and many times the buzz of the blue house fly. It was brown in color and striped with yellow, resembling an African *tsetse* with a sting no less sharp." The other complaint was about an insect "resembling a hornet only larger, and so savage and well-armed as to sting through the Captain's gaiter and send blood pouring into his shoe."[1]

The Englishman next turned his gaze on Brickell's store to watch, what seemed to him, the busiest spot in Miami. He wrote: "On the following day two canoes arrived at the store, containing two Indians and a squaw each, belonging to the remnant of the Seminoles who inhabit some of the 'islands' which rise above the Everglades and raise there corn, potatoes, and other vegetables, and animal skins, which they trade for their favorite 'fire-water.' These Indians lost no time in getting under the influence of the whiskey, and were dead drunk a few hours after their arrival."[2]

After staying only two days, the

Miami waterfront, c. 1900. Photograph by unidentified amateur.

The view was taken near the foot of Flagler Street, looking north. The steamer *City of Key West* (Miami to Key West Line), and the SS *Cocoa* (Miami to Nassau Line) can be seen in the distance at the Sixth Street dock.

Seminole Indian family and tourists, c. 1901. Photograph by unidentified amateur.

In later years, Musa Isle, a Seminole village about a mile up the Miami River, welcomed tourists collecting Indian souvenirs and photographs.

Seminole Indian family, Miami, c. 1901. Photograph by unidentified amateur.

One of several Indian families who frequented the area at the turn of the century.

172

Englishman felt well qualified to state his views on the good and the bad of life along the bay, make an assessment of Indian customs, and a survey of the landscape. He dismissed the area in his parting farewell: "As the season for hunting deer was over, we soon had enough of Miami and once more weigh anchor."[3]

Had the Englishman stopped by Miami a few years later, in the 1880s, he probably would have found things more to his liking, particularly if he had visited Cocoanut Grove, a new village along Biscayne Bay, just a few miles south of the Miami River. He would have found a hospitable and unpretentious hotel with good accommodations, operated by an English family, who, with a penchant for

Entrance to Fort Dallas Park, c. 1903. Photograph by Underwood & Underwood.

Over the years, the old Seminole War fort had crumbled and disappeared. In the 1890s, Mrs. Julia Tuttle acquired the property as part of her Miami real estate holdings. When she died in 1898, the property passed on to her son Harry Tuttle who, with his wife, lived on the estate when the above picture was taken.

Seminole Park, c. 1903. Photograph by Underwood & Underwood.

The "Old Officer's Quarters"

pioneering a new frontier, had no desire to return to the old sod.

The "Grove" was located across the bay from the old brick lighthouse on the south end of Key Biscayne. Looming tall on the horizon, the lighthouse made an excellent guide for vessels using the deep-water channel of Cape Florida when entering the bay from the ocean. At first, the colony at Cocoanut Grove was divided into two groups—the old-timers and the winter people. In time the two groups would become indistinguishable. The winter residents were an odd group of escapists from civilization, semi-wealthy, and united by the lure of sailboating—the bay being a paradise for small craft under thirty feet. On Washington's birthday in 1887, the Miami-Cocoanut Grove settlement held their first sailing race. The trading post owner William Brickell, an old-timer, if he could be called that, came in first. A few months

Residence on Southeast 2nd Avenue, between Flagler and Southeast 2nd streets, Miami, c. 1900. Photograph by unidentified amateur.

later, the Biscayne Bay Yacht Club was organized, perhaps an inkling that the utopian era for the free and easy life would not last much longer.

When Norton published his Florida guide book in 1890, transportation to Biscayne Bay was, as it had traditionally been, by foot along the beach or by schooner on the ocean. He wrote: "From Lake Worth to Norris Cut the beach offers but unsatisfactory foothold for man or beast. To the Hillsboro Inlet, about thirty miles from Palm Beach, the beach is unbroken; about half way is the Orange Grove house of refuge, where shelter, food and water may be obtained. Another house of refuge stands about seven miles before the New River Inlet is reached. The upper reaches of the river are very wild and beautiful. Eight miles south of New River Inlet is a 'haulover'...to Dumfounding Bay...thence to the headwaters of Biscayne Bay, about two miles, navigation is easy for small boats."[4] Norton made no mention of the pioneers and newly arrived homesteaders along the bay, but he said the hotel in Cocoanut Grove called Bay View charged ten dollars a week and that a good sized sloop or yawl, with two men, could be hired for fifty dollars a month, sailboats, for two dollars a day.

The Biscayne area began its Aladdin-like development in 1892, when the county decided to put through a road from Lantana to Lemon City. The road builder (and original promoter) became the owner of the stage line when the road was completed in 1893. Travel time by stage was two days each way—fare ten dollars one way, return sixteen dollars, with four dollars extra for "hotel" lodging at the New River stopover (each way). The hotel at Lemon City, if the tourist were going farther south on the bay, was more reasonable at two dollars per day. The following was written as a memorial by a tourist in November of 1893:

Looking up the Miami River, c. 1900. Photograph by Underwood & Underwood.

The river divided early Miami, and the new Flagler Street bridge (above, center) enabled the town to expand westward. Riverside, developed by the Tatum Brothers, was the first subdivision across the river.

THROUGH THE COUNTRY ALONG THE COUNTY ROAD BY HACK FROM LEMON CITY TO LANTANA

We commenced at Lemon City (population 90) on the Bay, taking notes as we ride up on the old trap, then called a hack, the motive power being mules that had not been curried since their arrival in Dade County, and had seemingly lost the devilish spirit supposed to be forever lurking beneath mule hide, ready to break forth at the most inconvenient time and tear things all to smash. These did nothing of the kind, but seemed on the point of lying down and going to sleep at any moment. It was a long and tiresome trip at best—sixty-three miles with little to relieve the eye, after having been over it once and having nothing new in the way of scenery to expect. The fact is, one really gets a very poor idea of the country as the road either follows on the high ridge next to the saw grass flats adjoining the ocean beach ridge, or is in the low beach scrub, only seeing good land when crossing streams.

Beginning, the first point reached is:

LITTLE RIVER

One and one-half miles from Lemon City, [Little River] is three miles long, narrow and deep; rises in Wood's Hammock from fine iron springs; it runs into the Bay. Four miles out and where we change mail is:

BISCAYNE BAY POST-OFFICE

This was one time the county seat, but now a few old timbers and some lime and lemon trees.

ARCH CREEK

Seven miles out. This is quite a curiosity and the stream is crossed on a natural stone bridge of solid lime stone.

LITTLE AND BIG SNAKE CREEKS

Ten miles out; flows into the Bay. Here we stop and eat dinner on the bridge. We don't think we ever saw so many trout and bream and such fine ones as would rush for crumbs of bread thrown over.

NEW RIVER

Our stopping place for the night, about 25 miles from Lemon City. Here is camp hotel, composed of a number of tents situated on the banks of the river and a most beautiful place. A post-office has been established here known as Fort Lauderdale.

NEW RIVER FIBRE FARM

This is an enterprise of a Jacksonville Corporation. Everything points to the ultimate success of the company who are pioneers in growing sisal for the market.

SNOW CREEK

Three miles from New River; empties into New River.

CYPRESS CREEK

Quite a stream, swift and deep, empties into Hillsboro River at Hillsboro Inlet.

HILLSBORO RIVER

Nineteen miles from New River and about the same distance to Lantana. Runs into the ocean about four miles from crossing.

INDIAN MOUND

A little over half way to Lantana from Hillsboro crossing will be seen the largest Indian mound in the state. In fact the largest of the many the writer ever saw.

[The account ends abruptly at this point. It is presumed that the writer reached Lantana safely.]

Halcyon Hall, architect's sketch, c. 1902. Photograph by Underwood & Underwood.

Located on East Flagler Street, halfway to the Bay, the structure was called "the prettiest in the State."

Advertisement from *History and Guide of Dade County, Florida*, 1896.

When the stage route to Lemon City opened in 1893, the picturesque era of the barefoot mailman had come to an end, the last link having been from Palm Beach to Biscayne Bay. Hardy tourists had often walked the beach south with the mailman and had listened to many stories about how travelers had lost their lives at shark-infested inlet crossings.

Another factor causing the Biscayne Bay frontier to crumble came in the fall of 1893, when the Florida East Coast and Transportation Company began dredging an inside waterway between Lake Worth and the bay. In the late 1880s, the company had already dredged a new canal between Mosquito Inlet and the Indian River and had since worked southward. Only the link south of Lake Worth remained to complete the inside waterway from Ormond and Miami. Two dredges, coming from opposite directions, met

**Florida East Coast Railway
brochure, 1900.**

to open the section between New River and Lake Worth in May of 1895, and as a result the steamer *Hattie* began regular service between Palm Beach and the settlement at Fort Lauderdale in August.

A month later, having completed road-bed grading and the building of bridges, workers began laying tracks southward from West Palm Beach for Flagler's railroad. During the same month, the dredge *Biscayne* was moving about 450 feet a day closer to the bay from New River. The race between the waterway and railroad was not unlike a gigantic tortoise and hare race—both contestants reached their goal about the same time in the spring of 1896. Tourists would now have the luxury of riding Palace cars for a straight run to Miami. Flagler owned the steamers, and they were not put into passenger service.

When it was first hinted that Miami might become a second Palm Beach, land buyers began looking about the bay area. In September of 1894, a Kentucky gentleman bought six acres of Miami bay-front property for $9,000, a high price, some thought. At this time, the future Miami area was primarily owned by two large landholders—Julia Tuttle with some 640 acres north of the Miami River, and William Brickell, who held about 2,000 acres south of the river along the bay. Ownership of Miami real estate completely differed from the situation Flagler had originally found at Palm Beach in the spring of 1893.

As the story now stands, the reason behind Flagler's decision to build his railroad to Miami and to open another luxury hotel was prompted by the big Florida freeze of late December, 1894, followed by another a few weeks later. Mrs. Tuttle, it was said, clipped a branch of green leaves, with fragrant orange blossoms, and sent it on to Flagler in St. Augustine. A timely reminder because the freeze in the ancient city had been a citrus disaster. Two years before, Mrs. Tuttle had tried to

interest Flagler in the Miami area and had apparently failed. At the time he was just embarking on the Palm Beach venture and had probably felt that one world at a time was sufficient. Evidently, by the winter of 1895, Flagler's outlook had changed due to the overwhelming success of his Palm Beach hotel and railroad.

The First National Bank, Miami, c. 1903. Photograph by Underwood & Underwood.

The bank opened on December 1, 1902. "Ask Mr. Foster" was a slogan well known to the later tourist of "boom-time" Miami. The two-seater Runabout (above, left) was probably Miami's first taxicab.

The First Presbyterian Church, Miami, c. 1900. Photograph by unidentified amateur.

The church and parsonage were one of Flagler's contributions to the city in 1899. They were conveniently located on East Flagler Street at the corner of Southeast 3rd Avenue, just a short distance from the Royal Palm Hotel.

The Royal Palm Hotel, Miami, c. 1902. Photograph by Underwood & Underwood.

"Its architecture is Italian Renaissance, or to use a more American term, Colonial, of perfect proportions.

The north and south facade is broken by pilasters and cornices finished in white, while the building is a deep cream with blinds of pearl gray." (From *The Tatler*, 1897.)

He was once again dreaming of pushing his empire southward.

In the early spring of 1895, Flagler contacted Mrs. Tuttle, and she agreed to give about half of her Miami real estate if, in return, Flagler would cut and pave the streets and make other improvements for the new city.

Dade County Court House, Miami, 1904. Photograph by Underwood & Underwood.

The Capitol Building Company had just put the finishing touches on the building when this photograph was taken.

Panoramic view from the Royal Palm Hotel, Miami, c. 1902. Photograph by Underwood & Underwood.

This view shows the most fashionable section of Miami at the turn of the century. Carriages for hire were waiting call on Southeast Third Avenue (foreground).

Meanwhile, Flagler's railroad had prospered and expanded. By the time the first train reached Miami in April of 1896, the list of its rolling stock was formidable—twenty-seven locomotives, five hundred freight and flat cars, fifteen baggage cars, twenty coaches, eight parlor cars, one private car (Flagler's), one business car, and four mail coaches, traveling over some 415 miles of track. The railroad's main office was centered at St. Augustine, as were other Flagler enterprises.

Early in 1896, Miami was a beehive of activity. The sound of hammers and saws pervaded the air as Mrs. Tuttle's hotel went up, along with many store buildings and homes. Work was started on Flagler's latest great hotel, and again a romantic name was chosen—The Royal Palm.

The Royal Palm was larger than the original Royal Poinciana at Palm Beach before its new wings were added; it measured 680 feet across its front with an attractive covered verandah about one-sixth of a mile around the outside, providing not only a fashionable promenade but a pleasant walk for the health seekers as well. The main entrance was imposing and stately, promising luxury and convenience. On entering the hotel, visitors were impressed by the vastness of the rotunda, which was like a great hall in Europe—an immense circular area two stories high, supported by Ionic columns forming arches leading to reception offices and newspaper and cigar stands. Beyond the arches, one side led to parlors and reading and writing rooms; the other

side, signaled by a formal row of Cor-
inthian columns, led to a magnificent
grand ballroom whose twenty-five-foot
ceiling was vaulted with small decorated
windows to admit light from above. Both
the rotunda and ballroom had massive
fireplaces with mantles and hearths of
native coral rock. A grand staircase with
two large upper landings rose from the
rotunda; each landing had two smaller
sets of stairs which led to the right and

**Near the mouth of the
Miami River, looking south
towards the bay, c. 1900.
Photograph by unidentified
amateur.**

**A small mountain of sand,
dredged from the bay, was
placed in front of the Brickell trading store (above,
far right). The "summer"
house overlooking the bay
was a retreat for guests staying at the Royal Palm Hotel.
A year or so later an open-
air addition to the shelter
was made.**

left wings, each containing guest rooms and other accommodations. Each of the Royal Palm's 450 tastefully furnished guest rooms was spacious, even for a luxury hotel, averaging twelve feet by eighteen feet and each with its own large closet. One hundred of these had private baths and each wing on both floors had two public baths. For the very wealthy, suites of rooms were available on the first floor.

A large dining room, tabled with fine china and white linen, was situated beyond the parlors on the first floor wing; leading from it were several private rooms and a children's dining room. For rainy or cool days, game rooms under the rotunda kept the guests from boredom.

The Royal Palm Hotel from the Miami River, c. 1901. Photograph by Underwood & Underwood.

"Here on a point formed by the meeting of the waters, on almost the same spot where old Fort Dallas stood, Mr. Henry M. Flagler has erected a handsome hotel of magnificent proportions." From *The Tatler*, 1897.

**The Miami River, 1903.
Photograph by Underwood
& Underwood.**

The hotel also had a separate building for service and maintenance. Located here were the boiler room, electric plant, kitchens, and ice-making apparatus. The kitchens were models of modern convenience. The chef's range was about forty feet long, and next to it was a smaller unit for cooking vegetables. A draft chimney directly above the ranges carried away all smoke and odors. The steam heat plant and laundry had five large commercial washers, two wringers, and two mangles. A staff of some three hundred people, including sixteen cooks, was needed to operate the hotel.

When Flagler left St. Augustine in February of 1897, en route to inspect his new Miami hotel, he traveled in a manner befitting a prince. A special train had been made up consisting of a baggage car, a parlor car, his private car *Alicia*, and a business car. Aboard the train when it left St. Augustine at 9 A.M. was his retinue of high officials and a few friends. The train stopped at Hotel Ormond where the party took a carriage jaunt through some pretty orange groves, followed by a delicious light lunch. The afternoon was spent traveling south, and the party arrived at the Royal Poinciana Hotel in Palm Beach at 5:30 P.M., where they put up for the night. In the morning, Flagler and his staff made an inspection of the casino, ocean pier, and bathing beach, and after lunch made an excursion on Lake Worth aboard a steam launch. At 3 P.M., they once again boarded the special train, arriving in Miami an hour later. At the Royal Palm a welcoming committee of well-polished employees awaited. Presumably the examination went well, because the next morning Flagler went up the Miami River to see the falls and to catch a glimpse of the Everglades.

Meanwhile, real estate prices had skyrocketed. A 50′ x 150′ lot on Flagler Street (12th Street) had gone up to $900, and on Miami Avenue (Avenue D) lots were selling for about $400.

The Golf Clock, Royal Palm Hotel, Miami, c. 1901. Photograph by Underwood & Underwood.

A putting green on the hotel grounds provided the less athletic golfers with exercise and an occasional wager.

From Florida East Coast Railway brochure, 1900.

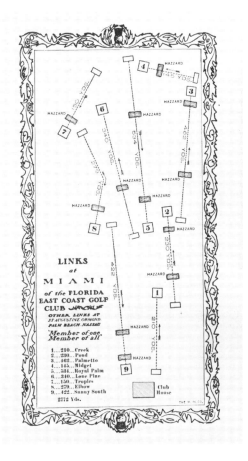

"The Golfing Fiend." The first tee, Miami, 1900.

"In Scotland golf is a recreation, dignified by age; in England and America it is a disease of the most virulent description. In his clothes, in his speech, in his manner, he stands revealed, and there is no mistaking him for other than what he is. Not the drink mania nor the bicycle craze marks its victims more plainly." (From *Munsey's Magazine*, 1896.)

Luxury houseboats on the Miami River, c. 1900.

"It is not surprising that in Florida we should find the highest type of houseboats....With a jolly company on board, the owner of a Florida houseboat snaps his finger at the crowded hotels and pursues his even way through the beautiful backwaters." (From *Munsey's Magazine*, 1906)

"The American Riviera," Royal Palm Hotel mooring, Miami River, 1902.

Originally, before Flagler and his men had initiated the Miami venture, they had, without doubt, investigated the advantages offered by Biscayne Bay as a deepwater port for steamships and large yachts. The United States Geodetic Chart for 1886 showed two relatively deep channels, Bears Cut and Cape Florida, with satisfactory depths. A third channel, Norris Cut, on the south end of future Miami Beach, also showed potential. Even before the Royal Palm was finished, a uniform nine-foot channel to the hotel was completed, and in early 1897 a turning basin was ready for large yachts coming in for the first season. In 1898, a channel was cut across the bay deep enough to accommodate large steamers and small steamships, thus enabling the Flagler empire once again to expand. By the turn of the century, the Florida East Coast Steamship Company was operating three tourist and pleasure boats out of Miami: The *City of Key West*; the *Miami* to Nassau; and the *Prince Edward*, to Havana.

Biscayne Bay had ideal docking facilities for large yachts like the *Boneta*, New York (above, far left). Stories about the wealthy in wintertime Florida were always worth repeating. It was a subject of gossip that "Pierre Lorillard's yacht *Caiman* was fitted with every convenience and luxury and was attended by a stable-boat which carried horses and carriages for the use of Mr. Lorillard and his guests."

A garden walkway, Miami area, c. 1900.

Hidden creeks with lush overgrowth of tropical vegetation gave tourists the feeling that they had entered a virtual Garden of Eden.

In addition to the scenic tropical beauties of the area, Miami had the advantage of a fabulous fishing ground around Biscayne Bay. In the winter of 1897, one of a party on the schooner *Privateer*, out for the day only, brought into the Royal Palm Hotel thirteen species of choice fish. The catch was a large one, as there had been a long warm spell. The thirteen varieties were placed on a tray on the hotel's counter. All had been caught in Bears Cut. The best catches were often found opposite Cutler about fifteen miles south of Miami and halfway across the bay.

From Fowey Rock Lighthouse, north, to the House of Refuge, could be covered in one day, trolling for kingfish, amberjack, and barracuda with a launch or by sailboat with a good wind. The visitor caught 135 kingfish in one day, and ten had lost all but their heads, by sharks. All in all, the Miami area was a fisherman's paradise. ■

The settlement on Indian Key, 1871.

"This picturesque island has a few of the old houses remaining that were built during the Indian war. At one time the whole place was burned and was the scene of a fearful massacre....It was the old story, whiskey and close bargains. The Indians were incensed and came in a body, burning and destroying....Dr. Perrine, a gentleman who located here for the purpose of pursuing studies in natural history, was burned to death in his house, his family escaping by boats." (Lithograph from *Harper's New Monthly Magazine*, 1871.

"Our Boat House," 1864, Dry Tortugas. Photograph by Joseph B. Holder.

It was here that Dr. Holder kept his boat between expeditions along the Florida reef to study the fauna and sea life so untouched in this wilderness far from the haunts of men.

During the Civil War years, when Key West and its outlying keys—the southernmost point of Florida—were off limits for tourists, the beauties of the area, the fauna, and the creatures of the sea were recorded in detail by Dr. Joseph Bassett Holder, zoologist and army medical doctor who, during the war years, was surgeon-in-charge at the United States military prison on Dry Tortugas. In a series of articles published by *Harper's New Monthly Magazine* in 1871, he wrote of not only Key West and Dry Tortugas but also the innumerable keys on both the east and west coasts of Florida. The Holder account would become a valuable travelogue for future tourists.

Dr. Holder had taken part in a government survey which made a reconnaissance of the great range of keys along the Florida Reef for the purpose of laying a cable from Cape Sable to Key West. The party's first stop after leaving Key West was Knight's Key, some sixty miles northeast, where they observed fragments of wrecks. After a short sail, they reached Boot Key, covered by beautiful groups of mangroves.

**Captain Jack's, Duval Street,
Key West, March, 1871.**

Captain Jack's "Gem" saloon (to the left above) was a favorite meeting place for the officers of the Navy and Army. The proprietor, a for- **mer Englishman, had once been a sailor, and he was considered by the towns-people to be a kindhearted man of good judgment.**

Fort Taylor, Key West, c. 1863. Photograph by Joseph B. Holder.

"Projecting from the seaward face of the town, Fort Taylor commands the entrance. A fine front of granite and brick work with castellated walls, [and] bastions." Although construction of the fort began in 1845, the disastrous hurricane of 1846 destroyed the preliminary work. However, it was ready for occupancy in 1861. Note the large sand banks thrown up early in the Civil War for protection against Confederate attack.

The next day the group crossed a channel to Matecombe Key, where two men who lived on the island told fearful stories, including one about a dog and a hog that were mutilated by a mysterious animal. Holder's party set up a night vigil in the hut, placing a board across the door and posting the cook as a look-out. The animal, a full-grown puma, or American lion, nearly five feet in length and standing over two feet high, came at midnight and was shot. The paws, heavy and powerful, measured four inches across.

On the following day the party explored Tavernier Creek, a favorite haunt for sea-turtles. During the breeding season "turtlers" plied their trade along the shore gathering green turtles for the Key West market. Also caught here was the hawk's bill turtle, its shell highly valued for jewelry and combs. Beautiful birds were in great abundance: great white herons, pelicans, gulls, and terns. Tourists often saw the bald eagle and osprey over-

The army hospital, Key West, c. 1865. Photograph by Joseph B. Holder.

head and an occasional scarlet ibis or roseate spoonbill.

The next morning the boat anchored off Old Rhodes Key, near Plantation Key, and everywhere along the beach lay parts of old wrecks—the remains of a steamship and figure-heads featuring handsomely carved scroll-work. On Plantation Key the owner of a large estate grew pineapples. At Key Largo, the next stop, mangroves grew close to the shore making it impossible to walk at the water's edge. The group also made a stopover at Indian Key, the grand rendezvous of the wreckers. Here boats for the sponge trade were built, and a few old houses remained from the time of the Indian Wars, when the island had been the scene of a bloody massacre. While on Indian Key, the Holder party responded to the islanders' call for "good old time scenes"—Jamaica rum, jigs and other dances to the tune of the violin. The villagers all gathered at the old store for the revel.

Man in boat. Key West in distance, c. 1867. Photograph by Joseph B. Holder.

United States Barracks, Key West, c. 1865. Photograph by Joseph B. Holder.

"The bay on the northern side bears a lively little fleet of vessels.... Opposite this bay is the government reserve, where is situated the United States barracks—an artillery post, and one of the neatest in the army. Six handsome cottages are arranged on two opposite sides of a square. Barracks for the privates are on the third side, facing the fourth, or front, which borders the bay. A handsome parade ground is within; and a hospital, with other appropriate quarters, is situated near."

Doctor Samuel A. Mudd, c. 1865. Photograph from Joseph B. Holder album.

Mudd was probably Fort Jefferson's best-known prisoner. He was convicted in the "Lincoln Conspiracy" in May of 1865 and sentenced to life in prison. President Johnson pardoned him in February of 1869.

From Indian Key, the survey party proceeded to the Cape Florida Light on Key Biscayne, where the group anchored after their two-week sail among the waters of the reef. After resting, they explored the mouth of the Miami River and visited Fort Dallas, with its neat cottage-barracks. On leaving Miami, they ranged down along the southern shore reaching Cape Sable, where large tracts of farm land made good profits for their Key West owners.

The wanderers now sailed along the west coast as far north as Cedar Keys. After exploring the waters of the Gulf and viewing a never-ending succession of birds, sea-creatures, and flowering plants, they turned homeward, and as they neared port, Holder recalled his entrance to Key West Harbor: "The Northwest Light twinkles an instant on the southern horizon, and disappears as the flush of the coming morn reveals its iron cage suspended in the broad space of waters. This is the entrace beacon of Key West Harbor, from the north. Our course is now clear for the low lines of waving tree-tops that mark our goal."[1] Holder was fortunate, as he had reached Key West just a few hours before the hurricane of 1865: "The rich azure of the sky is heightened to wondrous beauty by the moving volumes of day clouds; and the still sea mirrors the scene…as the day wanes the wreckers and the spongers make sail and stand in for an anchorage…a low line of leaden clouds lifts gradually at sunset and shuts in the richly colored scene."[2]

The party's boat, *Rosetta*, was wrecked by the storm, along with other considerable damage to shipping and town buildings. But this was only one of many storms to sweep the small town periodically over the centuries.

Key West, because of its temperate climate, attracted invalids. One visitor of 1838 who sought good health told of the town with its one hundred neat houses,

The George Ferguson house, corner of Caroline and Front streets, Key West, c. 1863. Photograph by Joseph B. Holder.

One of the richest men in Key West, Ferguson had a mill near the falls of the Miami River in the 1840-1860 era, where he manufactured *Ferguson's Florida Arrow Root*. The house was demolished when the Navy purchased the property in 1895.

fourteen stores, several warehouses, tavern, and courthouse. A meetinghouse was being built at the time of his visit, and a small Episcopal society met in the courthouse. He recalled only one boarding house with weekly lodgings available from $7.00 to $10.50. An abundant supply of turtle and fish provided adequate fare for the table, with an occasional shipment of vegetables and fruit from Havana. Fresh beef or mutton was nonexistent, although fowls were sometimes available. For amusement the town offered two billiard tables and a nine-pin alley. No horses or carriages were for hire, so walking was the order of the day. As for roads, a tolerable one led across the west end of the island and another along the beach to the east.

The visitor complained that he weighed seven pounds less after his stay and that the climate was too cold, although he did find several invalids from Pensacola and New York who had greatly improved. He also advised as to the best way to travel: "A good class of brigs run from New York to St. Marks twice a month touching at Key West."[3] Passage was forty dollars with ten dollars added from Key West to Havana, a better price than the Havana packets which charged seventy-five dollars for the trip.

The principal occupation of the town, from its beginning, was salvage or wrecking. Although many tourists, especially

"Old Fort Dallas," c. 1903. Photograph by Underwood & Underwood.

"This is the site of Fort Dallas. The block houses are now occupied as dwellings." (From Hawkes, 1869.) For awhile, prior to 1889, one room in the old stone barrack served as Dade County's courthouse. Improvements in the building were started in 1896.

Northerners, had supposed it to be a pirate's trade, wrecking was as legitimate as any other occupation, legally recognized with rules made for the mutual benefit of the wreckers, the wrecked, and the underwriters: "Those engaged in this are mostly men of wealth, character, of generous sentiments and human impulses. The rule among wreckers is, that he who first boards the wreck has control of her until delivered into the hands of the court. He determines, who, if any, shall aid him, and in what order and rate they shall share the benefits."[4] The disposing of salvage was determined by a court.

An interesting sidelight to the story is that many old-time sailors and wreckers of earlier days lived like hermits on isolated keys; they came to Key West for whiskey, their downfall, especially on a homeward-bound sail when the wind blew and the sea rose, thus thinning their ranks considerably over the years.

By 1852 nearly half of Key West's residents had come from the Bahama Islands. The Conchs, as they were called

Residence, Key West, c. 1865. Photograph by Joseph B. Holder.

"The profusion of flowering plants and trees impresses the stranger with pleasure. A stroll up and down the streets is quite enjoyable, particularly in the early spring, when there is rather more than the usual floral display. All through the winter plants bloom, birds sing, and insects flit and hum."

One of the interesting remarks made by Dr. Holder about the harbor and Fort Jefferson was that an aquarium had been built on the harbor side: "Concrete walls were built out fourteen feet into the water to form a square tank, the lower part being left in small crevices to admit freely the sea-water. The top of the wall was just above the surface, and wide enough to afford a comfortable standing-place where we could enjoy the pleasure of an exhibition... a most motely [sic] assemblage." Included among the tank inhabitants were crawfish, hermit crabs, fishes of all colors, sea anemones, members of the coral family, hammerhead sharks, cuttlefish, squids, conchs, etc.

**Joseph B. Holder, officers
and wives, Dry Tortugas,
1867.**

Before the fort was built, the Tortugas keys had been a rendezvous for pirates and had an unsavory reputation for stories of "Dead men tell no tales." To a first time visitor nearing Fort Jefferson by water, its battlements and towers and its lighthouse rising still higher seemed like a fairy scene, a floating castle.

During the Civil War years, prisoners of all kinds had thronged the fortress, and a little later the Lincoln conspirators, including the much maligned Doctor Mudd, came. Tales of cruel army officers, mistreated prisoners, and men dying of scurvy and yellow fever were later added to the stories of savage buccaneers and grisly tales of the sea.

After visiting Fort Jefferson, tourists found the Tortugas to be a land of infinite variety, including tropical heat if summer were near. Near the fort stood an abandoned hospital building, with crumbling walls and sagging roof—a curiosity shop for the inquisitive:

**View of Fort Jefferson, Dry
Tortugas, c. 1863. Photo-
graph by Joseph B. Holder.**

**The fort was an irregular
hexagonal structure of double circular walls of brick
and earth, with a founda-
tion of coral rock. Work on
the fort began in 1846, and
during the Civil War thousands of prisoners were
brought here. In 1869, two
steamers of the Alliance
line from Key West touched
monthly at the Tortugas.
Two schooners also plied
between the ports. Note the
arrangement of cannon-
balls in the foreground.**

because of their diving skills, were a hardy, industrious people who made a living diving into the holds of sunken vessels and under ships injured upon the reefs. A good working depth was from forty to fifty feet, but some were known to dive ninety feet to make fast anchors or for other necessary chores.

Sponging, a lucrative business, was another island activity of interest to travelers. After cleaning, drying, and pressing, the sponges were shipped to New York, and it was said that they were sold mostly to the French to make felt hats.

About sixty miles west of Key West lay a group of coral islands called the Dry Tortugas, with an elevation so low that one had a feeling of being in mid-ocean. Storms here were a strange and awesome experience.

Fort Jefferson, on the island of Garden Key, was always of interest to tourists.

View inside Fort Jefferson, Dry Tortugas, c. 1864. Photograph by Joseph B. Holder.

The officers' quarters may be seen to the rear of the lighthouse.

And in this room a tortoise
    hung,
An alligator stuffed, and other
    skins
Of ill-shaped fishes; and about
    his shelves
A beggarly account of empty
    boxes,
Green earthen pots, bladders,
    and musty seeds.[5]

Climbing up to the shop's shaky balcony, the tourist with a spyglass could survey a colorful scene of sky and sea. Just off the fort, monster sharks, some twenty to thirty feet long, slowly cruised back and forth around the area where blood and offal came from the slaughterhouse. For the naturalist, the distant whitish-blue of the sea revealed where creatures of the rock-like coral darted in and out of crevices, between beautiful white branches and leaflike forms, in the crystal clear water. Here, too, were large coral domes, not unlike Turkish minarets, where lurked angel and other tropical fish. Beyond was a distant shoreline, a bird watcher's delight, with Laughing Gulls, Monk's-heads, Black-caps, Red-bills, and many great Gray Gulls. Flying above were Frigate-birds hovering and swaying on their wide wings—the wreckers called them "Man o' War Hawks." For those who enjoyed literary settings from novels, there stood an old cottage, now in rubble, which James Fenimore Cooper described in his tale, *Jack Tier*.

If a tourist had a more active interest than a spyglass could satisfy, the rumor that the lighthouse keeper at East Key had found over one thousand dollars of silver money spurred many a treasure hunt on the Keys.

After the war, by 1869, Key West was ready for visitors with two hotels, the Russell House and the Florida House, both charging $2.50 a day or $40 to $60 a month. Also, three boarding houses were available. The houses in town were described as neat and attractive, and the lower part of town, called Conchtown, was a picturesque area where sponges decorated yards and fences. One visitor of 1869, after describing the virtues of the town,

Bringing in the turtle. Key West, April 1, 1885.

The huge turtle shown weighed in at 350 pounds. During the month of May, the turtlers sought their prizes. Some of the best specimens were found at East Key, the largest and outermost of the Tortugas, a dangerous area for shipping: "The turtlers camp here for the season. They make fast those that they catch, and send them into market as occasion offers. Some of these huge reptiles weigh over six hundred pounds and require all the strength of two men to turn them. When once on their backs, they are entirely helpless. As they are all females that come out of the water, they are allowed to lay their eggs before they are turned."

Fort Taylor, Key West, 1898. Photograph by Keystone View Company.

remarked on the moist air which "allows the moon and stars to shine with a rare and glorious brilliancy, such as we see elsewhere on dry and elevated plateaux."

By 1872, Key West had grown with a large trade in sponges, turtles, fruits, and cigar-making. Besides some twelve to fifteen cigar factories, there was also a factory for canning pineapples. Packet steamers brought tourists in from New York, New Orleans, Havana, Galveston, and Cedar Keys.

A visitor of 1881 recalled social life in the town. He said that a large and popular dance hall had a "cracked violin and piano."[6] In the heart of town was a roller-skating rink patronized by young people who glided about on skates or dashed about the outer edges of the rink on "swift-whirling" bicycles to the melody of the "Beautiful Blue Danube"—all to the perfume of orange blossoms, cape jessamine, and tuberose coming in with a delicious scent through the open doors and windows.

Key West did not change greatly in character as the century drew to a close. In the mid-1890s, after a tour of Florida, a group of photographers, en route to Cuba landed briefly at Key West: "As we were about to make a landing, the water on our side of the steamer was suddenly alive with small boys, white and black, ready to dive for money. They went down eagerly for silver pieces, but never saw copper....Everyone on board got off at Key West, happy to tread on terra firma, even if the dust was an inch thick.... It seemed to us a very uninteresting place, quaint but dirty...with more dust than anything else. We sailed from Key West that night at ten o'clock, taking the ninety miles to Havana leisurely, as no foreign vessel is allowed to enter the harbor before sunrise or after sunset."[7]

Dock at Fort Jefferson, Dry Tortugas, c. 1864. Photograph by Joseph B. Holder.

Boats at anchor. Key West Harbor, c. 1864. Photograph by Joseph B. Holder.

NOTES

Introduction

1. Because information about Florida photographers is not generally known or available, in a following section we have included, from our research files, brief biographies of photographers known to have worked in the state.

Chapter 1
Winter Migration

1. *Atlantic Monthly* (1876), pp. 29-32.
2. *Ibid.*
3. A.Q. Keasbey. *From the Hudson to the St. Johns.* (Privately printed by press of the New York *Daily Advertiser*, 1874), p. 7.
4. *Ibid.*
5. *Ibid.*, pp. 12, 13.
6. Charleston newspaper advertisement (1881-1882).
7. *South Florida Railroad. "Gate City" Route, Plant System, Sanford to Tampa.* (New York: South Publishing Company, 1887).
8. *Harper's New Monthly Magazine* (1884), p. 216.
9. *American Journal of Science and Arts* (January 1839), p. 64.
10. Unpublished manuscript by A.T. Havens, dating from December 30, 1842. (Courtesy of St. Augustine Historical Society.)
11. *Lippincott's Magazine* (1870), p. 605.
12. Scrapbook of D. Webster Dixon, dated November 25, 1875, p. 29. (Courtesy of Mrs. Kenneth Woodburn, Tallahassee, Florida.)
13. *Ibid.*, dated March 1876, p. 42.

Chapter 2
Fernandina and St. George Island

1. Ledyard Bill. *A Winter in Florida.* (New York: Wood & Holbrook, 1869), pp. 72, 73.
2. *Harper's New Monthly Magazine* (1878), p. 846.
3. *Ibid.*
4. *Illustrated American* (April 4, 1986).

Chapter 3
A Tour to Cedar Keys and North Florida

1. The spellings of Florida towns and geographic areas were always subject to change. Cedar Key, for example, was consistently referred to as Cedar *Keys* in nineteenth-century writings. In other instances, letters were often added or deleted, especially in Indian names, causing confusion to many authors of nineteenth-century books about Florida.
2. *Leslie's Popular Monthly Magazine* (1891), p. 217.
3. *Harper's Weekly* (1884), p. 692.
4. *Ibid.*
5. Sidney Lanier. *Florida: Its Scenery, Climate, and History* (Philadelphia: J.B. Lippincott & Co., 1876), p. 107.
6. *Winter from Home* (New York: John F. Trow, Printer, 1852), p. 37.

Chapter 4
Jacksonville

1. *All the Year Round* (London: 1885), p. 525.

2. *Ibid.*, p. 526.
3. *Harper's New Monthly Magazine* (1893), p. 494.

Chapter 5
The St. Johns River

1. Ledyard Bill, pp. 107-108.
2. *Harper's New Monthly Magazine* (1870), p. 657.
3. Unpublished manuscript by A.T. Havens, dating from December 30, 1842. (Courtesy of St. Augustine Historical Society.)
4. *The South: A Journal of Southern and Southwestern Progress.* (New York: The South Publishing Company, 1884). A newspaper.
5. *Ibid.*

Chapter 6
Along the Ocklawaha River

1. *Scribner's Monthly Magazine* (1874), p. 24.
2. *Harper's New Monthly Magazine* (1875), p. 162.
3. *Ibid.*, p. 166.
4. *Ibid.*, p. 166.
5. *Ibid.*, p. 167.
6. *Ibid.*, p. 171.
7. *Demorest's Family Magazine* (1893), p. 136.

Chapter 7
The Orange Belt

1. *Appleton's Journal* (1874), p. 593.
2. *South Florida Railroad. "Gate City" Route, Plant System, Sanford to Tampa.* (New York: South Publishing Company, 1887).
3. *Florida Times-Union* (February 18, 1887).
4. Charles Ledyard Norton, *A Handbook of Florida.* Part I. The Atlantic Coast (New York: Longman's, Green & Co., 1890), pp. 232, 233.
5. *Demorest's Family Magazine* (1893), p. 139.
6. *Leslie's Popular Monthly Magazine* (1891), p. 223.
7. George M. Barbour, *Florida for Tourists, Invalids and Settlers* (New York: D. Appleton and Co., 1883), p. 134.

Chapter 8
A Tour to Tampa and the West Coast

1. *Appleton's Journal* (1875), p. 258.
2. *All the Year Round* (London: 1885), p. 102.
3. *Ibid.*, p. 103.
4. *Ibid.*, p. 105.
5. *Scribner's Magazine* (1889), p. 159.
6. *South Florida Railroad. "Gate City" Route, Plant System, Sanford to Tampa* (New York: South Publishing Company, 1887).
7. *Demorest's Family Magazine* (1893), p. 135.
8. *American Amateur Photographer* (1895), p. 16.
9. *Leisure Hours in Florida on the West Coast Plant System,* (c. 1896). Brochure.
10. *Ibid.*
11. *Ibid.*

Chapter 9
St. Augustine

1. *Harper's New Monthly Magazine* (1874), pp. 171, 172.
2. *Winter from Home* (1852), p. 24.
3. *Ibid.*, p. 25.
4. Charles Hallock, *Camp Life in Florida: A Handbook for Sportsmen and Settlers* (Forest and Stream Publishing Company, 1876), p. 95.
5. A.Q. Keasbey, pp. 62, 63.
6. *Harper's New Monthly Magazine* (1875), p. 3.
7. *Ibid.*, p. 4.
8. *Ibid.*, p. 15.
9. *Scribner's Monthly Magazine* (1874), p. 12.
10. *Ibid.*, p. 14.
11. Charles Norton, p. 172.
12. *Demorest's Family Magazine* (1893), p. 140.

Chapter 10
Along the Halifax River

1. From an old quotation found in a Maine newspaper, (1841).
2. *Harper's New Monthly Magazine* (1893), p. 506.
3. *Boston Home Journal* (January 28, 1888).
4. Letter from Mrs. Henry Ward Beecher. Reprinted in Ormond Hotel Booklet, (1889).
5. *Demorest's Family Magazine* (1893), p. 137.
6. *Harper's New Monthly Magazine* (1893), p. 506.

Chapter 11
Indian River Country

1. Charles Hallock, p. 212.

Chapter 12
Palm Beach

1. Charles Norton, p. 223.
2. *Munsey's Magazine* (1902), pp. 331, 332.

Chapter 13
Miami

1. *Appleton's Journal* (1875), p. 335.
2. *Ibid.*
3. *Ibid.*
4. Charles Norton, p. 226.

Chapter 14
The Keys

1. *Harper's New Monthly Magazine* (1871), p. 706.
2. *Ibid.*
3. *A Winter in the West Indies and Florida*. By an Invalid. (New York: Wiley & Putnam, 1839), p. 128.
4. *De Bow's Review* (1852), p. 414.
5. *Harper's New Monthly Magazine* (1868), p. 262.
6. James A. Henshall, M.D., *Camping and Cruising in Florida* (Cincinnati: Robert Clarke & Co., 1884), pp. 177-180.
7. *American Amateur Photographer* (1895), p. 16.

SELECTED BIBLIOGRAPHY

Adams, J.S. *Florida: Its Climate, Soil, and Productions, with Sketches of Its History, Natural Features and Social Condition.* Jacksonville: Edward M. Cheney, State Printer, 1869.

All the Year Round (London). 1885.

American Amateur Photographer, The. 1895.

American Journal of Science and Arts, The. 1839.

Ancient City, The. 1850-1854.

Appelton's Journal. 1870, 1875.

Atlantic Monthly. 1876, 1879.

Bacon, Eve. *Orlando: A Centennial History.* Chuluota, Florida: The Mickler House Publishers, 1975.

Barbour, George M. *Florida for Tourists, Invalids and Settlers.* New York: D. Appleton and Co., 1883.

Bill, Ledyard. *A Winter in Florida.* New York: Wood & Holbrook, 1869.

Bloomfield's Illustrated Historical Guide. St. Augustine: Max Bloomfield, 1885.

Bowe, Richard J. *Pictorial History of Florida.* Tallahassee: Historical Publications, Inc., 1965.

Brevard County, Florida or The Indian River Country, 1889.

Brinton, Daniel Garrison. *A Guide Book of Florida and the South.* Philadelphia: Penn Publishing Co.; Jacksonville: Columbus Drew, 1869.

British Journal of Photography, 1886.

Brown, S. Paul. *The Book of Jacksonville.* Poughkeepsie, New York: A.V. Hoight, 1895.

Browne, Jefferson B. *Key West: The Old and the New.* Reprint of the 1912 edition. Gainesville: University of Florida Press, 1973.

Business Directory, Guide and History of Dade County, Fla. for 1896-97. West Palm Beach: C.M. Gardner and C.F. Kennedy.

Cadwell, Roy. *Clearwater: "A Sparkling City."* Minneapolis: T.S. Denison & Company, Inc., 1977.

Cantrell, Elizabeth A. *When Kissimmee was Young,* 1948.

Century Magazine. 1893.

Chautauquan, The. 1884-1890.

Cohen, Isidor. *Historical Sketches and Sidelights of Miami, Florida.* Miami: 1925.

Corse, Carita Dogget. *The Key to the Golden Islands.* Chapel Hill: The University of North Carolina Press, 1931.

Darrah, William Culp. *Stereo Views.* Gettysburg: Times and News Publishing Co., 1964.

————. *The World of Stereographs.* Gettysburg: W.C. Darrah, Publisher, 1977.

De Bow's Review. 1852.

Demorest's Family Magazine, 1893.

Dewhurst, William W. *The History of Saint Augustine, Florida.* Reprint from 1885 edition. Rutland, Vermont: Academy Books, 1968.

Dunn, Hampton. *Re-Discover Florida.* Miami: Hurricane House Publishers, Inc., 1969.

East Florida Herald, 1845-1848.

Field, Henry M. *Bright Skies and Dark Shadows.* New York: Charles Scribner's Sons, 1890.

Florida: A Guide to the Southernmost State. New York: Oxford University Press, 1939.

Florida Herald and Southern Democrat. 1839-1849.

Florida Historical Quarterly. July, 1975.

Florida Mirror, The. 1877.

Florida Sentinel. 1843-1854.

Florida Times-Union (Jacksonville). 1883-1900.

Floridian, The. 1845-1860.

Frisbie, Louise. *Peace River Pioneers.* Miami: Seemann Publishing Inc., 1974.

Gardiner, R.S. *A Guide to Florida: "The Land of Flowers."* New York: Cushing, Bardua & Co., 1872.

Godown, Marion and Rawchuck, Alberta. *Yesterday's Fort Meyers.* Miami: E.A. Seemann Publishing, Inc., 1975.

Gold, Pleasant Daniel. *History of Volusia County Florida.* DeLand: The E.O. Painter Printing Co., 1927.

Gonzalez, Thomas A. *The Caloosahatchee River.* Privately printed, n.d.

Graff, Mary B. *Mandarin on the St. Johns.* Gainesville: University of Florida Press, 1963.

Gregg, William H. *Where, When, and How to Catch Fish on the East Coast of Florida.* Buffalo and New York: The Matthews-Northrup Works, 1902.

Grismer, Karl H. *Tampa.* St. Petersburg Printing Company, Inc., 1950.

Groene, Bertram H. *Ante-Bellum Tallahassee.* Tallahassee: Florida Heritage Foundation, 1971.

Guide to Southern Georgia and Florida. Savannah: Atlantic and Gulf Railroad, 1879.

Hallock, Charles. *Camp Life in Florida: A Handbook for Sportsmen and Settlers*. Forest and Stream Publishing Company, 1876.

Hanna, Alfred Jackson and Hanna, Kathryn Abbey. *Florida's Golden Sands*. Indianapolis and New York: The Bobbs-Merrill Company, Inc., 1950.

         Lake Okeechobee. Indianapolis and New York: The Bobbs-Merrill Company, Inc., 1948.

Harper's New Monthly Magazine. 1868-1871, 1874, 1878, 1884, 1893.

Harper's Weekly, 1884.

Havens, A.T. Unpublished manuscript. New York: 1842.

Hawks, J.M. *East Coast of Florida*. Lynn, Massachusetts: Lewis and Winship, 1887.

Hebel, Ianthe Bond, ed. *Centennial History of Volusia County, 1854-1954*. Daytona Beach: College Publishing Company, 1955.

Henshall, James A., M.D. *Camping and Cruising in Florida*. Cincinnati: Robert Clarke & Co., 1884.

Hine, C. Vickerstaff. *On the Indian River*. Chicago: Charles H. Sergel & Company, 1891.

Holden, Luther L. *Guide to Florida*. By "Rambler." New York: The American News Company, 1875, 1876.

Illustrated American. 1896, 1897.

Jacksonville, Florida and Surrounding Towns, 1889-90.

Keasbey, A.Q. *From the Hudson to the St. Johns*. Privately printed by press of the Newark *Daily Advertiser*, 1874.

Knickerbocker New York Monthly Magazine, The. 1836, 1839, 1843.

Lanier, Sidney. *Florida: Its Scenery, Climate, and History*. Philadelphia: J.B. Lippincott & Co., 1876.

Leisure Hours in Florida on the West Coast Plant System: The Weal and Wonders of the Peninsula as Seen by Maj. C.H. Smith (Bill Arp). c. 1896.

Leonard, Irving A. *The Florida Adventures of Kirk Munroe*. Chuluota, Florida: The Mickler House Publishers, 1975.

Leslie's Popular Monthly Magazine. 1891.

Lippincott's Magazine. 1868, 1870, 1875.

Lorant, Stefan. *The New World: The First Pictures of America*. New York: Duell, Sloan & Pearce, 1946.

MacDowell, Claire Leavitt. *Chronological History of Winter Park, Florida*. Privately printed, 1950.

McDuffee, Lillie B. *The Lures of Manatee*. Nashville: Marshall & Bruce Co., 1933.

Maloney, Walter C. *A Sketch of the History of Key West, Florida*. Reprint of the 1876 edition. Gainesville: University of Florida Press, 1968.

Martin, Richard A. *Eternal Spring*. St. Petersburg: Great Outdoors Publishing Co., 1966.

Martin, Sidney Walter. *Florida's Flagler*. Athens: The University of Georgia Press, 1949.

Munsey's Magazine. 1902.

Norton, Charles Ledyard. *A Handbook of Florida*. Part 1. The Atlantic Coast. New York: Longman's, Green & Co., 1890.

Ober, F.A. *The Knockabout Club in the Everglades*. Boston: Estes and Lauriot, 1887.

Outing, The. 1890.

Parks, Arva Moore. *The Forgotten Frontier*. Miami: Banyan Books, Inc., 1977.

Peters, Thelma. *Lemon City*. Miami: Banyan Books, Inc., 1976.

Peterson's Magazine. 1891.

Pierce, Charles W. *Pioneer Life in Southeast Florida*. Coral Gables: University of Miami Press, 1970.

Pizzo, Anthony P. *Tampa Town 1824-1886*. Miami: Hurricane House Publishers, Inc., 1968.

Popular Health Resorts of the South. St. Augustine: Chapin & Co. Publishers, 1885.

Powell, Evanell Klintworth. *Tampa That Was*. Boynton Beach: Star Publishing Company, Inc., 1973.

Prince, Richard E. *Atlantic Coast Line Railroad*. Green River, Wyoming, c. 1966.

Reynold's Standard Guide, 1890.

Rinhart, Floyd and Marion. *The American Daguerreotype*. Athens: The University of Georgia Press, 1981.

Scrapbook of D. Webster Dixon. (Courtesy of Mrs. Kenneth Woodburn.)

St. Augustine Daily Herald. 1898.

St. Augustine Examiner. 1859-1869.

St. Augustine, Florida. Compiled by John F. Whitney, ed. and proprietor, Florida Press, 1873.

St. Augustine News, 1838-1845, 1888.

St. Nicholas Magazine. 1894.

Scribner's Monthly Magazine. 1874.

Sewall, R.K. *Sketches of St. Augustine.* Reprint from the 1848 edition. Gainesville: The University Presses of Florida, 1976.

Smiley, Nixon. *Yesterday's Miami.* Miami: E.A. Seemann Publishing, Inc., 1973.

The South: A Journal of Southern and Southwestern Progress. New York: The South Publishing Company, 1884.

South Florida Railroad: "Gate City" Route, Plant System, Sanford to Tampa. New York: South Publishing Company, 1887.

Tampa Guardian, The. 1880.

Tatler, The. 1891-1897.

Torrey, Bradford. *A Florida Sketch-Book.* Cambridge: The Riverside Press, 1894.

Travers, J. Wadsworth. *History of Beautiful Palm Beach.* Private printing by author, 1928.

Windhorn, Stan and Wright, Langley. *Yesterday's Key West.* Miami: E.A. Seemann Publishing, Inc., 1973.

Winter at Ft. George, Florida. Published by the Fort George Island Company, 1887.

Winter from Home. New York: John F. Trow, Printer, 1852.

A Winter in the West Indies and Florida. By an Invalid. New York: Wiley and Putnam, 1839.

BIOGRAPHIES OF PHOTOGRAPHERS

The following is a list of professional and amateur photographers who practiced the art in the state of Florida from 1842 until 1900. The information is limited to existing citations obtained by the authors; thus, it is highly probable that a gallery or vendor was in operation before or after the dates indicated. For ease of referral, the biographies of photographers and those of the vendors of photography have been combined under one listing.

Key to abbreviations for sources of research are as follows:

AD	Floyd and Marion Rinhart, *The American Daguerreotype*, 1981
APB	*Anthony's Photographic Bulletin* for date noted
BD	Business directory or register for city and date noted
CD	City directory for date noted
Dag'typist	Daguerreotypist
FU	*Florida Times-Union* (Jacksonville) for date noted
Nsp	Newspaper for the city and date noted
P	Extant print
PP	*Philadelphia Photographer* for date noted
Photog'r	Photographer
SBD	State business directory for date noted
SG	Extant stereograph (stereo view)
SV	William Culp Darrah, *Stereo Views*, 1964
SW	William Culp Darrah, *The World of Stereographs*, 1977
T	*Tatler, The* (St. Augustine) for date noted
USC	United States census for year indicated

Abbott, W.R. Photog'r. Quincy, Florida, 1889. SBD.

Akerly, Mary. Photog'r. Took view in 1895 of the Ocklawaha River, Florida; sailed on "Okeehumkee," from Palatka to Silver Springs. Wrote article with photographic illustrations. *The Photographic Times*, 1895.

Allen, Charles. Photog'r. Born Oct. 1862, Ill. Tarpon Springs, Florida, 1900. USC.

Allen, C.J. Photog'r. 9½ Romana St., Pensacola, Florida, 1911. CD.

Alvord, Kellogg and Campbell. Photog'rs. 57 Bay St., Jacksonville, Florida, 1878. SG; SV.

America Illustrated. Stereo view publisher; issued reprints in the 1870s, including Tropical Series, Florida Views. SG; Green Cove Springs, c. 1873; SV.

American Scenery. Stereo view publishers; issued reprints in the 1870s, including Florida views. SG, Enterprise, c. 1876; SV.

American Stereoscopic Company. Stereo view publisher, 853 Broadway, New York, N.Y.; issued stereographs after 1865, including Florida views. SG; Silver Springs, c. 1880; SV.

Anthony, E. (Edward) & H.T. (Henry T.) Co. Stereo view publisher and distributor. American and Foreign Stereoscopic Emporium, 308 Broadway (after May 1, 1860, at 501 Broadway), NYC. Thomas C. Roche, Anthony's staff photographer, took views in Florida before 1874. Published as a series—Jacksonville, St. Johns River, St. Augustine, Ocklawaha River, Silver Springs, Green Cove Springs, Magnolia, etc. Edward Anthony—Pioneer dag'typist, manufacturer, wholesaler of photographic materials. Born 1818, NYC; died 1888. Leading co. in photographic supplies, 1850s. Produced carded paper print stereo views (1859), taken by the company's staff of photog'rs and until about 1875 was the country's largest producer of stereo views. By 1870, the largest photographic stock establishment in the world. Henry T. Anthony—civil engineer, inventor, manufacturer of photographic supplies, amateur photographer. Born 1814; died 1884, NYC. In charge of manufacturing division of E. Anthony & Co., NYC, 1852–1860, and E. & H.T. Anthony & Co., NYC, 1860 onward. Member of eclipse expedition, 1869. AD.

Armstrong, John. Photog'r. Born Aug. 1855, Illinois. Listed as a "photographic artist," Wauchula Precinct, De Soto Co. (Fort Green), 1900. USC.

Ashbrook, Eura M. (single female). Photog'r. Born July 1876, Ky. Tampa, 1900. USC.

Ashmead Bros. Distributor of Florida views. Listed 33 West Bay St. Jacksonville, 1879 and later. FU; CD.

Aten, Isaac. Photog'r. Pine Castle, Orange County, 1885. Taking ferrotypes. *The Photographic Times & American Photographer*, p. 338.

"B" (Best) series. Stereo view publisher; issued good quality reprints in the 1870s, including Florida views. SG, Green Cove Springs, c. 1874.

Bailey, James. Dag'typist. Rooms over Barnard's Drugstore, Tallahassee, 1853; Kuhns and Bailey, Tallahassee. Advertised "long experience in the art, prices 10% over New York," 1854. Advertised "ambrotypes and melainotypes taken by Bailey." Refitted rooms over Barnard's Drugstore, Tallahassee, 1857. Nsp.

Barker, George. Photog'r. specializing in stereo views. Niagara Falls, N.Y., c. 1860–1900. Best known for his views of Niagara Falls. Took views in many localities across the country, including Florida. In 1888 at the National

Photographic Association convention at Minneapolis, he displayed a number of interior views for which he was given a first medal—these were views of Southern hotels, principally the Ponce de Leon, St. Augustine. Took large views of the "Oldest House," St. Augustine, c. 1887, in both plain and hand-colored, 17″ x 20″. (Examples at St. Augustine Historical Society.) Awarded many medals over the years—special prize silver medal, Germany, 1886; special grand prize of a diamond badge at the Photographer's Association of America convention, 1887; gold medal at Boston; gold medal in summer of 1889 at Paris Exposition for his collection. APB (1888), p. 488; SG, Green Cove Springs, c. 1886; Indian River, c. 1889; SG, copyrighted views of oranges, pineapples, etc., south Florida, 1890s; *Photographic Times* (1890), p. 111.

Barnes, J.E. Photog'r. Barnes Photographic Parlors, Hudnall Block, Orange Ave., Orlando, 1890. Nsp.

Bass, Richard H. Photog'r. Born 1877, Florida. Jasper, 1900. USC.

Bell, Henry L. Photog'r. Born 1871, Florida. Pensacola, 1900; gallery 1911 at 14½ S. Palafax St. USC; CD.

Bennett, Nathan S. Dag'typist. Boston, Mass., 1844. Took daguerreotypes of Florida's Seminole warrior Billy Bow Legs, c. 1852. CD; *Humphrey's Journal*, v. 5, 1853; AD.

Berth, James W. Photog'r. Born 1846, Pa. Greenville (Madison Co.), 1880. USC.

Bickel, W.P. Photog'r. Cedar Key, 1886, 1889. Also see Wood and Bickel. SBD.

Bien, E. & Co. Photog'r(?). Palatka, 1870. SG.

Bierstadt, Charles. Photog'r. Niagara Falls, N.Y. Born Germany, c. 1828; died Niagara Falls, 1903. Immigrated to New Bedford, Mass. c. 1832. With brothers, Albert (artist) and Edward, took up photography in 1850s. Entered photography partnership with Edward late 1850s; dissolved 1867. Moved to Niagara Falls, 1867; made stereo views including Florida. Considered one of America's finest stereo scene photographers. Sold negatives to E. & H.T. Anthony and Underwood & Underwood. SG, Silver Springs, c. 1879; SG, St. Augustine, c. 1880. Also see Robert Taft, *Photography and the American Scene* (Dover reprint ed., 1964); SV.

Billinghurst, C.J. Photog'r. McArthur, Ohio, 1869. Orange Heights, Florida, 1893. PP, p. 221; wrote article on tintyping for *Photo Mosaics*, 1893, pp. 102–103.

Blackman, Leslie A. Photog'r. Born June 1867, Ga. Lake City, 1900. USC.

Blair, Lewis W. Photog'r. St. Augustine, 1911. CD.

Bloomfield, Max. Stereo view publisher. Born Germany. Immigrated to U.S., 1877. Issued reprints. Published *Bloomfield's Guide* with list of stereo views offered, 1883–1886. Also newsdealer and Florida curiosities vendor. St. Augustine, c. 1880–1887. SBD; CD; SG; Guide; FU; USC.

Bogert, Ity, Miss. Photog'r. Born 1867, NYC. Okahumpka (Lake Co.), 1900. USC.

Bonine, E.A. Photog'r. Jacksonville, 1871 (Views in the Sunny South, Florida Series); Jacksonville, 1872 (Florida views in Centennial). Pasadena, Calif., 1880s. SG; SW.

Bonine, R.K. Photog'r. Tyrone, Pa. Published various stereo views under "Globe Photo Art Company," including Florida, 1890s. SW.

Borthe, William. Photog'r. Born Germany, 1791. Ocala, 1880. USC.

Brockway, John R. Photog'r. Born 1840, N.Y. Jacksonville, 1880. USC.

Brooks, Miss Beck. Amateur photog'r. Took photographs 4¼″ x 3½″ in Ocala and St. Augustine, winter of 1891. P.

Brooks, Hiram N. Photog'r. Born 1858, Ga. La Villa (Duval Co.), 1880. USC.

Brown, George. Photog'r and artist. Long's Blocks, St. Augustine. Advertised life-size portraits from small size, 1889; St. Augustine, c. 1890; 27½ E. Bay Jacksonville and St. Augustine, c. 1900. Used "air brush process." SG, view of St. Johns River, 1885; SBD; SG.

Brown, George W. Photog'r and ferrotyper (tintypes). Itinerant. Tent in rear of courthouse, almost opposite the old post office "as cheap as can be procured in Savannah." Tallahassee, 1875. Nsp (Sept. 21). (Courtesy of Dorothy Dodd.)

Browne, J.N. Photog'r. Born 1855, New York, N.Y. Jacksonville, 1886. USC.

Brownson, N. Photog'r. Stereo views. Fernandina, 1870s. SW.

Brydges, J.G. & Sons. Photog'r. From Pa. "View of the Fire at Ocala," Ocala, 1884. Nsp, *The South*.

Buell, O.B. Photog'r. Key West, c. 1875. SG.

Buky, Jessie D. Photog'r. Born 1878, Ky. Palatka, 1900. USC.

Burgert, James. H. Photog'r. Born Sept. 1876, Ohio. Tampa, 1900. USC.

Burgert, Jean E. Photog'r. Born Dec. 1879, Ohio. Tampa, 1900. USC.

Burgert, Samuel P. Photog'r. Born 1840, Ohio. Listed 79½ W. Bay, Jacksonville, 1883; 71½ W. Bay, Jacksonville; Tampa, 1886. Studio, later known as Burgert Brothers, Tampa, 1886–1940 and after. Also see sons: James, Harry, Jean E., Walter, and William. FU; SBD; USC.

Burgert, Walter. Photog'r. Born Dec. 1881, Ohio. Tampa, 1900. USC.

Burgert, William. Photog'r. Born 1875, Ohio. Tampa, 1900. USC.

Bushnell, J.H. Dag'typist. Itinerant, Miss., Ga., Florida. Tallahassee, Nov. 28, 1848, "will remain a few Days"; advertisement, Dec. 12, "children 5 to 8 seconds, prices $2–$6 according to size." Quincy, Florida, Dec. 23, 1848. Left Tallahassee, Dec., 1849. Probably the same J.H. Bushnell who managed the Florida House, St. Augustine, July 1851. AD; Nsp. (Courtesy of W. Robert Nix and Dorothy Dodd.)

Campbell, Alfred S. Photog'r. St. Augustine, 1896. SG, St. Augustine City Gates, copyrighted, 1896.

Cannon, John W. Photog'r. Deland, 1884. "The leading and only Photographer in Deland." Lived on a 14-acre orange grove just out of town. *The South*, 1884.

Chamberlain, J.N. Photog'r. From Woonsocket, Rhode Island. Photographed *Nantucket Illustrated*, copyrighted 1888 by Wittemann. 28 albertypes. Springfield House (Nantucket) reproduced in Floyd and Marion Rinhart, *Summertime* (Clarkson N. Potter, 1978). Miami, 1896 (?); Miami, 1902. *Munsey's Magazine*, v. 28; Glimpses of Miami, Florida, copyrighted 1904. 33 photogravures.

Chapin, George H. Photog'r(?). Museum Bldg., St. Augustine. Advertised stereo views, 1873–75; St. Augustine, 1885. *The Rambler*; *Chapin's Guide Book*.

Choate, J.N. Photog'r. Carlisle, Pa. Took views of St. Augustine, c. 1870. P.

City Gate Photographer. Tintyper. St. Augustine, c. 1895; City Gate Studio, 1907–08. CD; SG.

Clover, G.H. Photog'r. 11 Masonic Temple, Pensacola, Florida, 1911. CD.

Clumker, John. Photog'r. Born 1852, Germany. Came to U.S., 1876. Naturalized citizen. Milton, Florida, 1900. USC.

Colby, Charles Harrison. Photog'r. Ocala, 1889–1895. A photograph, "The Boat Landing, Blue Springs," by Colby was illustrated in *Mosaics*, 1893. Colby also leader of a fifteen piece orchestra which played at Ocala's principal hotel. "Ocala's popular photographer" died on August 3, 1895. SBD; SW; *Wilson's Photographic Magazine*, May 1890, 1895.

Cole, H.S. Photog'r. Deland, 1886, 1889. SBD.

Cooley, Sam A. Photog'r. Official photog'r U.S. Army, Dept. of the South. Took views of Jacksonville and St. Augustine, 1861–1865. *The Photographic History of the Civil War*, 1912.

Cottrell, Charles. Photog'r. Born Aug. 1863, Ala. So. Polifax St., Pensacola, 1900–1911. USC; CD.

Cox, William A. Photog'r. Born 1842, Md; died St. Augustine, 1914 (Evergreen Cemetery). St. George St., St. Augustine, 1878; St. George Street, St. Augustine, 1885–1900; residence at Marine St., 1886; 14 Sevilla St., 1899; 170 St. George St., St. Augusitne, 1911–1912. SG; USC; CD; SBD.

Crane, Henry L. & Son. Photog'r. Formerly Mann & Crane. Tampa, 1857. Nsp.

Crawford, P.J. (and wife). Photog'rs. Ft. Meade (Polk Co.), c. 1880s. (Courtesy Joan Morris.)

Curtiss, G. Amateur photog'r. Belonged to Jacksonville Camera Club, 1893—"some views of Florida oranges and live oaks." *The Photographic Times & American Photographer*.

Cushing, W.H. Photog'r. Cushing's Southern Scenery. Probably winter itinerant. Took views of Jacksonville and Palatka, c. 1870; Palatka, c. 1871–1872; Palatka and St. Augustine, 1875; Wedding scene, Palatka, Apr. 4, 1876. SG. (Courtesy Joan Morris.)

Dakin, Leonard. Amateur photog'r and banker. Born upstate N.Y. Dakin & Son, Orange Grower, Racimo (near Georgetown). Took views of Florida life at Racimo, Georgetown, and vicinity, c. 1884–1895. Edward Steichen wrote "contributes a unique document to the Americans of his time." Pauline Dakin Taft, *The Happy Valley*, 1965. (Courtesy Joan Morris.)

Darnell, W.W. Photog'r. Gainesville, 1889. SBD.

Davis, E. Jeff. Photog'r. Bought out Moore Bros. studio, Jacksonville, 1909. *Bulletin of Photography and Photographer*, 1909.

Davis, G.W. Photog'r (Davis Photographic Gallery). Born N.Y., 1824. Jacksonville, 1888–1894. B.W. Jackson, manager 1889. USC; P; SBD; FU.

Dean, Charles A. Amateur photog'r. Winter visitor from Boston. Photographed around Punta Gorda, Pine Island, Fort Meyers area with a Kodak "Pull the string, press the Button" (3″ round), 1887–1910.

Dewall, C.M. Photog'r. Born 1848, Florida. Beacon St., Jacksonville, 1880; Orlando, 1886; Orlando, 1889. USC; SBD.

Douglas, James. Photograph vendor. 46 East Bay, Jacksonville, 1885; 1889–1901 at 23 E. Bay St.; 1902 at 429 W. Bay St.; SBD.

Douglass, W.H. Dag'typist. Albany, N.Y., 1850. Gallery, St. Louis, Mo., 1852; moved to Florida, 1853. AD; Missouri Historical Soc.; *Humphrey's Journal*, 1853.

Dowd, Thomas P. Photog'r. Born Vermont, 1868. St. Augustine, 1900. USC.

Drew, H. & Bros. Vendors of Florida views and albums. 59–61 W. Bay St., Jacksonville, 1889–1892. Advertised in 1892 that Kodaks and photographic supplies were stocked. FU.

DuBose, Henry B. Photog'r. Born Mar. 1870, Ga. Forsyth St., Jacksonville, 1900. USC.

Ducros, Louis. Artist and photog'r. Born Aug. 1851, France. Immigrated 1871. Residence 1324 S. Ft. Harrison Ave., Clearwater, 1890s; Bellair town, 1900. Photographed the 1891 Clearwater fire on Cleveland St. Commissioned to document the construction of the Belleview Biltmore Hotel, 1896. Nsp; USC.

Duganne & Callison. Photog'rs. Gainesville, 1880s. SV.

Dykes, Isaac W. Photog'r. Born Ala., 1864. Bonifay (Holmes Co.), 1900. USC.

Elliot, H.J. Photog'r. Pensacola, 1903. CD.

Engle & Furlong. Photog'rs. Fernandina, c. 1877, c. 1880. SG.

Enseminger Bros. Photog'rs. J.A. Enseminger. Born Ashland (?), Ohio, 1843. Moved to Florida from Iowa, 1885. Sanford, 1886; Park Ave., Sanford, 1900. Took view of Ft. Meyers, late 1880s; views of Jacksonville, 1901. SBD (Ohio); SBD; USC; Library of Congress. (Courtesy Joan Morris.)

Estaves, Andrew (Esterez, Andreas). Photog'r. Born Cuba, 1849. Immigrated, 1869. Naturalized. Key West, 1880; Duval St., Key West, 1900. USC.

Estada, Hermenyeldo (?). Photog'r. Born Mar. 1867, Spain. Immigrated, 1892; naturalized. 17th St., Tampa, 1900. USC.

Eutslear, R.E. Dentist and photog'r. Sumterville, 1886. SBD.

Farmer, Charles. Photog'r. Born Mar. 1865, Ga. Bridge St., Jacksonville, 1900. USC.

Fenton, A.K. Photog'r. Anclote, 1889. SBD.

Field, A.S. Photog'r. Born 1841, Ohio. Lake City, 1868–1878; Lake City, 1880. SV; USC.

Field, James C. Photog'r. Born Feb. 1845, Ohio. New Gallery, corner Lafayette and Franklin streets, May 1, 1882. Advertised: "Pictures taken by dry plate process—Views of buildings, groups, etc. Taken in town or country. Old pictures copied." Tampa, 1883. Landscape photographer. "Will go to any part of the state to make views under contract. Florida views of all kinds for sale." Franklin and Twiggs St., 1886; Photog'r and Havana cigar dealer, Tampa, 1889; Tampa, 1900. SBD; Nsp; USC.

Florida Club, The. Photog'rs. A group of Boston photographers wintering in St. Augustine, whose stereo views were published by Charles Pollock of Boston. St. George Street, St. Augustine, 1868–c. 1878. SG, various views in and around St. Augustine, some dated 1870–1875; SV; SW; SG shows Florida Club headquarters on St. George Street.

Florida Photographic View Co. Marshall (A.H.) & Dobbins (A.N.). A.H. Marshall, from Ohio. 24 W. Bay St., Jacksonville, 1882–1885. CD; SBD.

Frear, W.H. Dag'typist. Itinerant. Room at Mrs. Gues Bldg., corner Bridge and Charlotte streets, St. Augustine, 1850. Montgomery, Ala., 1854. AD; Nsp; SBD (Ala.).

Frederick, William D. Photog'r. Born Aug. 1856. Tarpon Springs, 1900. USC.

Freeman, G.P. Photog'r. Born Feb. 1859, Ga. Bartow, 1886; 1889, 1900, 1907, 1908. SBD; USC.

Freidal, C. Dag'typist, from N.Y. In Representative Hall of Capitol, Tallahassee, 1852—"In town for a few days." Nsp.

Gardner, M.M. & W.H. Photog'rs. 13 Marietta St., Atlanta, Ga., and Carpenter Grove, Orange City, Florida, c. 1883–84; Florida views, Orange City, c. 1890. SV; SW; BD (Ga.).

Gault, S.W. Photog'r. Jacksonville, 1859; Keogh's House, Bay Street, St. Augustine, Dec. 1859. Advertised pictures any style, moderate price. A beautiful selection of stereoscope pictures for sale. Nsp.

Geer, L.H. Photog'r. Died Orlando, 1903. Court St., Orlando, 1884; Orlando, 1886. *The South* (1884); SBD.

Gems of Florida. Stereo view vendor or publisher(?) National Hotel, Jacksonville, c. 1878 or before. SG.

Goode, E. Photog'r. Lakeland, 1886. SBD.

Gore, O.M. Photog'r. Helena, 1886 (Helena was six miles east of Live Oak, later deserted). SBD.

Gottleib, Harry J. Photog'r. Born 1874, N.Y. Monticello, 1900. USC.

Granger, J.B. Photog'r. Waldo, 1886. SBD.

Grant, Alonzo G. Photog'r. Florida Photograph and Ferrotype Co., Bay St., Jacksonville, 1875; Box 723, Jacksonville, and Thomasville, Ga., c. 1881–1883, and later. Advertised "Largest collection of Stereoscopic slides, and large views of Florida Life and Scenery…enters into contracts to illustrate Estates, Railroads, etc. Florida Land Agency Booklet (1875). SG, number of views of northern and central Florida; SW.

Graves, Carlton H. Photog'r and publisher. "Universal Photo Art Company," Philadelphia. Florida views, 1896–1904. SG; SW.

Gray, Anna B. Photog'r (with husband Edward H.). Born 1871, Ohio. Branford, 1900. USC.

Gray, Edward H. Photog'r (with wife Anna B.). Born 1868, Ohio. Branford and Iverness, 1900. USC.

Green, George W. Photo-engraver. Born May 1866, England. Immigrated 1868. Newman St., Jacksonville, 1900. USC.

Gridley, Horace Warren. Photog'r (amateur). From England (visitor). Took views of northern Florida, c. 1886. *British Journal of Photography* (Oct. 29, 1886).

Griffith and Griffith. Stereo view publisher. The photog'r William H. Rau, of Washington, D.C., supplied a number of their Florida views. Home offices—St. Louis, Liverpool, England, etc. SW; SG, steamer Okahumpkee on the Ocklawaha, c. 1900.

Haas, Isaac. Photog'r and taxidermist. Green Cove Springs, 1878–1898. *Anthony's Photographic Bulletin* in 1886 list of 5″ x 8″ Florida scenery (p. 360). APB; SBD; SW.

Halton, Fountain J. Photog'r. Born 1866, Florida, Madison, 1900. USC.

Hand, Fred. Photog'r. Born 1860, Germany. Immigrated 1876. Titusville, before 1894; Clematis Ave., West Palm Beach, 1894–1896; 4th St., Miami, 1900. Nsp; BD; USC.

Hankins Thomas. Itinerant dag'typist. Pavilion opposite Mrs. Dresdales, St. Augustine, 1850. Also, Nashville, Tenn., date unknown. AD; Nsp; extant dag'type. (Courtesy of Robert Cauthen.)

Hardman, A.S. Photog'r. Leesburg, 1889. SBD.

Harper, Alvan S. Photog'r. Born 1846, Norristown, Pa.; died May 19, 1911. Moved to Philadelphia, c. 1849. Philadelphia photog'r, 1875–1885. South Monroe St., Tallahassee, 1885–1886; moved studio near home on Green Square, Tallahassee, 1889. SBD. (Courtesy Joan Morris.)

Harris, Edward G. Photog'r. Born 1853, Ill. Daytona Beach, 1888, 1890. Orange Ave., Daytona Beach, 1900. P, steamer *Rockledge*; USC. (Courtesy Jacqueline Bearden.)

Hartley, L.J. Photog'r. Longwood, 1886. SBD.

Havens, O. Pierre. Dag'typist (?), photog'r. Born Sept. 1837, N.Y. Began photographing about 1856. Rumored to have taken a photograph of Lincoln, c. 1860. Sing Sing, N.Y. before 1874. Wilson (J.N.) and Havens, 141 Broughton St., Savannah, Ga., 1874–1876; 141 Broughton St., Savannah, Ga. (alone), 1877–1886; 67 & 69 W. Bay St., Jacksonville, 1887–1908. Havens became the leading Florida photog'r in the 1890s. He pioneered and advertised platinum photographs in 1895; probably the highest quality photographic prints ever offered to the public. Also introduced an unknown process called the "Carbonnette," 1896. Advertised "babies as quick as a wink." Proclaimed one of America's leading photographers, he won first and second prize medals for excellency, Photographic Assoc. of America, 1894–97. Well-known nationally for an issue of 25 stereo views of Sing Sing prison, 1873. Also wrote articles for *The American Annual of Photography*, 1890, and *Photographic Times Almanac*, 1889. CD (Ga.); SBD (Ga.); USC; Nsp; CD; SBD; P; SG; APB.

Hensley, J.W. Photog'r. Lake City, 1886. SBD.

Heslop & Iles. Ambrotypists. From Charleston. Jacksonville, November 1, 1860. Nsp.

Higgins, A. Photog'r. Welshton (midway between Ocala and Lake Weir), 1886. SBD.

Hill, Charles. Photog'r. Key West, 1889. SBD.

Hine, Thomas A. Amateur photog'r. From Newark, N.J. Spent winters on shores of Biscayne Bay. Member Newark Camera Club, 1889. *Photographic Times & American Photographer.*

Hines, Otto. Photog'r. Took views in Florida, 1885. APB.

Hobbs, Carter R. Dag'typist. Over Haywood's Book Store, lately occupied by Bushnell, Tallahassee, Jan. 1, 1849. Nsp.

Holder, Joseph Bassett. Zoologist, medical doctor, author, amateur photographer. Born Lynn, Mass., Oct. 26, 1824. Entered U.S. Army, and from 1860–1867, surgeon-in-charge at the U.S. military prison at Tortugas, Florida. Photographed at Dry Tortugas and Key West. In 1870 became curator of invertebrate zoology, icthyology, and herpetology in the American musuem of natural history, N.Y. Author of several books including *History of the North American Fauna*, 1882; *History of the Atlantic Right Whales*, 1883; *The Living World*, 1884. *Appelton's Cyclopaedia Biography*, 1888.

Hooven, D.F. Photog'r. St. Augustine, c. 1890. P.

Hoover, Joe C. Photog'r. Born 1879, Iowa. Starke, 1900. USC.

Howard, Clarence C. Photog'r. Born Sept. 1858, Pa. Orlando, 1900. USC.

Huber, E.L. Photog'r. Eustis, 1886. SBD.

Hunt, G.H. Photog'r. Born Oct. 1846, Ind. Key West, 1900. USC.

Hunton, F.N. Publisher, stereo views. Sold Florida views, Gem Series. Jacksonville, 1876. SG.

Hylton, W.O. Dag'typist. Born Jamaica, B.W.I.; died Feb. 27, 1857. Tallahassee, 1852–1853. Nsp.

Ingersoll, Orden L. Photog'r. Born Nov., 1865, Mo. Tenth Ave., St. Petersburg, 1900. USC.

Jackson, Edward. Photog'r. Born May, 1855, Ga. Whitehead St., Key West, 1900. USC.

Jackson, William H. (W.H.J. & Co.) Photog'r. Born 1843, McKeesville, N.Y.; died 1942. Considered finest of American nineteenth-century landscape photographers. Accompanied the Hayden survey of 1870, following roughly the old Oregon Trail, as official photog'r. Photographed the West and western Indians during the 1870s. Commercial photog'r in the 1880s and later. Studio at Denver, Colo., late 1880s, when Jackson made his first trip to Florida. Photographed scenes mostly on the east coast of Florida. Displayed photographs at the Philadelphia Photographic Society, 1890: "W.H. Jackson, of Denver, was represented by some of his superb views of Florida and other sections. Altogether, this display was worth a day's vacation to see it and study the marvelous effects obtained on these wonderful plates" (APB, 1890, p. 587). Returned to Florida in 1894 and photographed the Royal Poinciana Hotel, Palm Beach; photographed the fresco art work on the interior ceilings and other points of interest around the Ponce de Leon Hotel and vicinity of St. Augustine. A number of his views of Florida were copyrighted, and many, beautifully tinted, were sold in St. Augustine in the 1890s. P; T; Robert Taft, *Photography and the American Scene*, 1964; Ralph W. Andrews, *Picture Gallery Pioneers*, 1964; *Sunlight Pictures*, 1895.

Jacoby, W.H. Artist and publisher. Minneapolis, Minnesota, 1868–c. 1880. Florida views. S; SV.

Jaggard, Randall. Dag'typist. Rooms formerly occupied by John R. Lloyd, Tallahassee, 1852. Nsp.

Johnson, Melvin F. Photog'r. Born 1856, N.Y. Hawthorne town, 1900. USC.

Jones, Edgard. Photog'r. Born 1865, Ohio. St. Augustine, 1900. USC.

Kauffman, L.O. Photog'r. Pensacola, 1905. CD.

Keystone View Co. Publishers of national and international stereo views, including Florida. Founded 1892 by B.L. Singley; employed a number of unidentified photog'rs, and later acquired negatives from competing stereo publishing concerns. Published a number of Florida views between 1900–1910, stamped "copyright" without specifying date. SG; Robert Taft, *Photography and the American Scene*, 1964; SV; SW.

Kilburn Bros. Photog'rs and publishers. Edward, dag'typist and, after 1865, print technician. Benjamin, photog'r; died 1909. Littleton, N.H., 1865–c. 1900 and later. The company issued nature themes, historic places, scenes of America, and views of foreign countries. SG, Ocklawaha River, c. 1880; SG, Tallahassee, c. 1882; SV.

Kitchell, J.G. Amateur photog'r. Tampa. *Camera Mosaics*, 1894.

Klunker, John. Photog'r. Pensacola, 1903–1911. CD.

Knabe, G.J. Photog'r. Born 1873, Germany. Immigrated 1894. E. Bay St., Jacksonville, 1900. USC.

Knott, C.B. Amateur photog'r and general superintendent of the Florida East Coast Railroad Hotel System. Three views of Ormond appeared in *Photo-American*, 1897, pp. 190, 331.

Kuhn, William. Dag'typist, photog'r. Tallahassee (Kuhn and Bailey), 1854; "leaving city for a few weeks, Tallahassee, 1856," Tallahassee (Kuhn only), 1867. Announced that he would be in Tallahassee for a few days taking photographs, ferrotypes, etc., Feb. 17, 1874. Nsp; BD. (Courtesy Dorothy Dodd.)

Lane, Charles A. Photog'r. Made photogravures from negative of Cocoanut Grove at Lake Worth (printed by N.Y. Photogravure), 1890. *Sun and Shade*, Nov., 1890.

Lansing, Alfred A. Wood engraver, itinerant dag'typist. Probably the first dag'typist to come to Florida. Son of Garret Lansing, one of America's earliest engravers on wood. Alfred Lansing was said by the historian Lossing to have been the first to engrave large pictures for circus and theatre bills. Also a comic actor. Advertised as "Professor of photography. Only one minute's sitting required. $5—Hours 9–4." Itinerant with rooms at St. Augustine's City Hotel, April 1842. Nsp; Groce and Wallace, *The New York Historical Society's Dictionary of Artists*, 1957.

Launey, Arthur R. Photog'r. Savannah, c. 1880–1895. Partnership with George C. Goebels, 1890–1895 when partnership dissolved. Then operated at "The Studio." Advertised Florida stereo views for sale. SG; CD; Nsp.

Laurens, Peter. Dag'typist. Itinerant. Office at Mr. Brush's Boarding House, St. Augustine, Jan. 1844. Nsp.

Leach, William. Photog'r. Baltimore, Md., 1860s. St. Augustine, c. 1885. PP; SG; CD.

Lee, N.B. Photog'r. Born 1875, Va. Punta Gorda, 1900. USC.

Legg, C.J. Photog'r. Winter Park, 1886. SBD.

Legg, F.W. Photog'r. Winter Park, 1886. SBD.

Lester, B.J. Dag'typist. Phoenix Bldg., Tallahassee, 1848; Albany, Ga., (Mar. 29); Tallahassee (Sept. 7), 1850; winter 1850–51, Tallahassee. Nsp. (Courtesy Dorothy Dodd.)

Lloyd, John R. Dag'typist. Rooms over Ball and Pratanes Clothing Store, Tallahassee, Oct. 1850; Lloyd & Perkins (J.W.), Tallahassee, Nov. 20, 1850; Lloyd & Jaggard, Tallahassee, Oct. 1852. Nsp. (Courtesy Dorothy Dodd.)

Lonewell, S.J. Photog'r. Helena (six miles east of Live Oak), 1886. SBD.

Longwood, Van. Photog'r. Born 1864, N.Y. St. Augustine, 1900. USC.

Lyon, A.T. Photog'r and ambrotyper. Tallahassee, 1859. Purchased gallery of James Bailey. Formerly with Tucker & Perkins, Augusta, Ga. Nsp. (Courtesy Dorothy Dodd.)

McCarthy, W. "Portrait Agent." Born July 1865, Ill. West township, Key West, 1900. USC.

McIntyre, G.A. Dag'typist, dentist. Rooms at Mrs. J.L. Denilly's, Tallahassee, 1844, 1845. Nsp.

McIntyre, Sterling C. Dag'typist, dentist. Adv. as dentist with G.A. McIntyre, Mar.–Sept., Tallahassee, 1844. Adv. as dag'typist, Nov. 10, 1844, Tallahassee; adv. Jan. 28, 1845, "taking colored Daguerreotype Likenesses in the latest style and will continue, as heretofore, the practice of Dentistry in all its branches." Adv. in the *Florida Sentinel* May 13, 1845, that he would be in Marianna about the 20th for a few days and then proceed to Pensacola. Gallery at 190 & 200 King St., Charleston, S.C., 1847–1848. To Tallahassee, 1848. Adv. that he would be ready to execute likenesses about Dec. 16 in the old office of the *Sentinel*. An item in *The Floridian* on Feb. 3, 1849, informed the public that he was leaving for Key West. Listed at 663 Broadway, NYC, 1850–51. To San Francisco sometime during 1850. Took panorama of San Francisco in early 1851. AD; Nsps. (Also information courtesy Joan Morris and Dorothy Dodd.)

McLeed, H.S. Photog'r. Born 1852, Ga. Tampa, 1880. USC.

Mancel, Henry. Photog'r. Born Jan. 1839, France. Immigrated 1863. Naturalized. 15 E. Intendencia, Pensacola, 1886, 1889, 1897, 1900. SBD; USC.

Manerly, Harry. Photog'r. Born Nov. 1859, S.C. Gadsen St., Pensacola, 1900. USC.

Mangold, Jonas G. Photog'r. Palatka and Moline, Ill. Views of Rock Island City, Davenport, Moline and vicinity. Palatka, 1870s. Lost everything in fire, "will take views of same," Palatka (Mangold & Sons), 1893 and later. SG; SW; P (copyright, 1893).

Marshal, S.H. Photog'r. Born 1832, Tenn. Lived in Ohio, 1880; came from Ind., 1883. Jacksonville, 1885. USC.

Mears, J.F. Photog'r. Florida views. Palatka, c. 1872–79. SG.

Melson, F. Photog'r. Sanford, 1889. SBD.

Meriwether, H. Photog'r. Leesburg, 1886. SBD.

Merrill, Genevine H. Photog'r. Born 1878, Iowa. Palatka, 1900. USC.

Merwin, John. Photog'r. Born 1857, N.Y. New Smyrna, 1900. USC.

Miller, Wellie (single female). Photog'r. Born 1846, Iowa. Eustis, 1900. USC.

Milling, George. Photog'r. Born Mar. 1874, Ga. Sixth Ave., St. Petersburg, 1900. USC.

Mitchell (J.S.) & Dewall (C.M.). Photog'rs. See individual listings. Jacksonville, 1870s. SW.

Mitchell, J.S. Photog'r. Born 1845, Portland, Me. Boston, 1865. 77½ W. Bay St., Jacksonville, 1881, 1885, 1886. SBD; USC.

Mitchell, James. Photog'r. Born 1866, Florida. Jasper, 1900. USC.

Moffat Bros. (E.F. & C.S.B.). Photog'rs. In 1860 the *American Journal of Photography* stated that Moffat of Key West sent a sample of sea island cotton to the editor—"skillful and intelligent adept in photography," (p. 224). Key West, 1886; 1889; 1900. SBD.

Monroe, Ralph. Amateur photog'r. Early pioneer settler. Took views around Cocoanut Grove, Miami, in the 1880s, 1890s, and later. Founder of the Biscayne Bay Yacht Club. Anna Moore Parks, *The Forgotten Frontier*, 1977.

Moore, Jackson D. Photog'r. Born 1851, Florida. Orange Co., 1880. USC.

Moore, R.A. Photog'r. Born Mar. 1873, N.C. Forsyth St., Jacksonville, 1900. USC.

Morgan, Rufus. Photog'r. Stereo views. New Bern and Morgantown, N.C. Photographed cities and towns of the South and elsewhere. SW; SG, Palatka, c. 1872.

Morrow, Stanley J. Photog'r and ambrotyper. Born May 3, 1843, Richmond Co., Ohio; died Dec. 10, 1921, Dallas, Tex. Joined 7th Infantry, Wisc. Vols., Civil War. Studied photography under Matthew Brady. Opened gallery in Yankton, Dakota Territory, 1867. Taught wife photography. Traveled through the Dakotas and upper Missouri country. Unable to accompany Custer and 7th Cavalry because supplies did not arrive in time, May 1876. Official photog'r to General G.A. Crook and later Indian campaigns, 1876–1877. Moved to Geneva, Florida, 1882. Worked for South Florida Railroad as photog'r with views reproduced in Plant booklet of 1887. Also, photographed for the South Publishing Co., NYC. Moved to Atlanta, Ga., in 1888; opened studio at 30 Whitehall St. briefly. Office at same address selling disinfectants and deodorizers, same year; 148 Whitehall (home); vice-president ODD Co. (disinfectants), 1889. Travel agent, same address, 1890. Many of Morrow's negatives of the West and Indians were lost in a Jacksonville fire soon after he moved to Atlanta. *Coronet* (magazine), Apr. 1939. Robert Taft, *Photography and the American Scene*; CD (Atlanta). (List courtesy Joan Morris.)

Mullikin, John. Photog'r. Born 1874, S.C. Tallahassee (unemployed), 1900. USC.

Mullikin, William. Photog'r. Born 1876, S.C. Tallahassee (unemployed), 1900. USC.

Murphy, Henry. Itinerant photog'r. Gallery over Mr. Bonkin's store. One dozen good pictures, $2.50—Mar. 23—last week in Tallahassee, 1875. Nsp. (Courtesy Dorothy Dodd.)

Myer, J.F. Photog'r. Born 1846, S.C. Orange Co., 1880. USC.

Naturalist in Florida, The. Probably a publisher (C.J. Maynard.) Established, St. Augustine, 1884. SG.

Neck, Reubin. Photog'r. Born Florida, 1880. Palatka, 1900. USC.

New York Studio. Photog'r. City Gate, St. Augustine, c. 1900. P.

Nielson & Co. Mfr. of paper and glass views, Niagara Falls, N.Y. View of Ocklawaha River, c. 1890. P.

Ober Bros. Photog'rs. Fernandina, 1870s. Inland river stereo views, new series, c. 1882. SW; SG.

Ober, Charles K. Photog'r. (Ober Bros.) Beverly, Mass. Fernandina, 1870s, c. 1882. (Courtesy Joan Morris.)

Ober, Frederick. Photog'r. (Ober Bros.) Tallahassee, 1876—"the celebrated photographic artist…photographing the different places of interest in this section of the state." Nsp. (Courtesy Dorothy Dodd.)

O'Keefe, C.F. Photog'r. Madison, Ohio. St. Augustine, c. 1890. SG; P.

Owens & Woodward. Photog'rs. Ocala, c. 1900. P.

Owens, Luther. Photog'r. Born Nov. 1857, Ga. Marion St., Tampa, 1900. USC.

Pacetti, Gabriel. Photog'r. Born 1843, Fla. St. George Street, St. Augustine, 1880, 1886. USC; SBD.

Palmer, P.L. Dag'typist, dentist. Tallahassee, 1850. Nsp.

Parlow, Gevit. Photog'r. Born Apr. 1837, Mass. Franklin St., Tampa. USC.

Paxton, A.B. Photog'r. Eustis, c. 1878; Gulf Key, 1886. SG; P; SBD.

Pender, Herbert. Photog'r. Born Feb. 1865, N.C. Lakeland, 1900. USC.

Perkins, J.W. Photog'r. See Lloyd & Perkins.

Pierron, George. Photog'r. Born 1816, France. Marine Street, St. Augustine, 1870–1880; St. George Street, St. Augustine, 1883–1889. USC; SBD; CD.

Pinard, Felix. Photog'r. Born 1845, France. Immigrated 1880. Naturalized. Sarasota, 1900. USC.

Pinardo, F. Photog'r. Born Dec. 1844, France. Immigrated 1869. Naturalized. Ollivette St., Tampa, 1900. USC.

Pine, F.B. Photog'r. Stereo views, St. Johns River, c. 1878–c. 1898. SV.

Pine, George. Photog'r. Born January, 1835, N.J. Trenton, N.J., used paper negatives (100) for scenes of Florida, winter of 1885–1886 (Eastman Dry Plate Co. Booklet, 1886); Brookville, 1900. USC.

Pine, R.G. Photog'r. Gulf Key, 1886. SBD.

Power, Edmund. Photog'r. Born May 1837, Ireland. Immigrated 1887. Dunnellon, 1900. USC.

Price, G.L. Photog'r. Born 1849, S.C. Gainesville, 1870. USC.

Randall, C.E. Photog'r. Tallahassee, 1886. SBD.

Rau, William H. Photog'r and publisher. Philadelphia and Washington, D.C. Also sold negatives to other publishers. SG, Ocklawaha River, c. 1892.

Renshaw, R. Photog'r. Palatka, 1884, 1886. Fire records, Palatka; SBD.

Resler, Richard E. Photog'r. Born March 1865, Austria. Immigrated 1867. West Palm Beach, 1900. USC.

Reymond, J.P. Amateur photog'r. From Detroit, Mich. Member Detroit Amateur Photograph Society; displayed views near Gainesville and St. Johns River. *Camera Mosaics*, 1894.

Roberts, David. Photog'r. Born June 1828, Ga. Near San Mateo (Putnam Co.), 1900. USC.

Roberts (J.L.) & Cole (N. Byrd). Photog'rs, ambrotypers. Old Kuhn's Gallery, next to telegraph office, Tallahassee,

1871. Nsp. (Courtesy Dorothy Dodd.)

Roche, Thomas C. Photog'r, inventor. Died Oct. 22, 1895, NYC. Staff photog'r for E. & H.T. Anthony. Famous for views of West. Took many stereo views of the South, including Florida, 1870s. APB (1895), p. 367.

Rodugues, Avalardo. Photog'r. Born January 1876, Florida. Nephew of Andrew Estaves. Duval St., Key West, 1900. USC.

Rogers, Marcus H. Amateur photog'r. A winter visitor from Mass. Former editor. Took views of St. Lucie Wharf, Indian River, and St. Augustine, 1886. Photograph in *Anthony's Photographic Bulletin*, 1887, p. 73; *British Journal of Photography*, June 1886.

Ryan, David J. Photog'r. Born 1837, Ireland. Savannah, Ga. 1870–1880. Advertised Florida and Georgia scenery. USC; S; PP.

Sache & Potter. Photog'rs and ambrotypers, tintypers. From Galveston, Tex. "Pictures taken on patent leather, convenient for sending letters," Tallahassee, August 1859; Skylight gallery—"will remain during hot season," Tallahassee, November 13-December 25, 1860. "Photographs (18″ x 20″) of the members of the convention and ordinance of secession…accompanied by a key giving the name of each delegate. $5.00 each." Nsp.

Sala,   . Photog'r. Pensacola, 1897. *Bliss' Quarterly* 1897.

St. Claire, Stewart. Photog'r. Born 1849, Scotland. Jacksonville, 1880. USC.

Sanders, D. Photog'r. Born 1872, Ky. Jacksonville, 1900. USC.

Sanders, George R. Photog'r. Born January 1858, Sweden. Immigrated 1860. Bluff Springs (Escambia Co.), 1900. USC.

Scadin, R.H. Amateur photog'r. From Dexter, Mich. Photographed St. Johns River, etc., in 1893. Photographs in *Camera Mosaics*, 1894.

Scholze, J.J. Photog'r. Born 1854, Austria. Immigrated 1882. Naturalized. Bowling Green (De Soto Co.), 1892; Braidentown (Bradenton), 1900. P; Nsp; USC.

Schoon, A.V. Photog'r. Silver Spring Park (5 miles north of Ocala), 1889. SBD.

Scott, Andrew. Dag'typist, and ornamental plasterer. Died, 1843. Formerly of Baltimore. Tallahassee, 1843. Nsp.; (Courtesy Dorothy Dodd.)

Seaver, C. Jr. Dag'typist, photog'r. Stereo views published by Chas. Pollock, Boston. Gallery Boston, 1854-1864 and later. Traveled New England, South, and West, 1865-1875 (?). Took views of Florida along the St. Johns River, The Southern Series, 1870-1875. AD; BD; SG; SV; SW.

Sedgwick & Vannerson (Julius Vannerson, Washington, D.C.), 1853-1858 (?). Photog'rs. St. Augustine, 1886. SBD.

Shear, S. Photog'r. "The Indian River Photographer." Cocoa, Rockledge, Melbourne, late 1880s, 1889, 1891. Probably took stereo views along the N.J. Coast, c. 1880. SG, *On the Indian River*, C.V. Hine, frontispiece; P.

Shear (W.B.) & Flournoy (J). Photog'rs. De Funiak Springs, 1889. SBD.

Shen, Seath. Photog'r. Born 1851, N.Y. Beach St., Daytona City, 1900. USC.

Shubert,   . Pensacola, 1897. *Bliss' Quarterly*, 1897.

Sills, Jervis. Photog'r. Born Sept. 1870, Ga. E. Romcina Ave., Pensacola, 1900. USC.

Singley, B.L. Photog'r and publisher. Stereo views, Meadville, Pa., 1892 onward. National and international views. Large range of subjects including Florida views. SG, Indian River, copyright, 1893; SG, Key West, copyright, 1898; SV; SW.

Smith, James H. Photog'r. Born 1853, Ohio. 77½ W. Bay, Jacksonville, 1889; Gainesville, 1900. SBD; USC.

Smith, Norton & Co. Music dealers and photograph vendors. "25,000 views on exhibition, also large assortment of Florida views." Corner Newman and Forsyth St., Jacksonville, 1875; *Florida* (Florida Land Agency booklet), 1875.

Snow, Miss S.B. Amateur photog'r. Portsmouth, N.H. Exhibited, third Annual Society of Amateurs, Boston, 30 prints of Florida. *Photographic Times & American Photographer*, 1886.

Souter, J.L. Photog'r. Green Cove Springs, 1886. SBD.

South Publishing Co., The. Photo-engravers. NYC., 1886. SBD.

Spaulding, J.M. Dag'typist. Tallahassee, 1849. Nsp. (Courtesy Dorothy Dodd.)

Spencer & Armour. Photog'rs. St. Lucie (Brevard Co.), 1877. P, Jupiter lighthouse.

Stephens, Evanton. Photog'r. Born 1851, Ga. Orange Town (Liberty Co.), 1900. USC.

Stephens, W. Dutchman. Photog'r. Born 1880, Ga. Orange Town (Liberty Co.), 1900. USC.

Stockton, Telfair. Newsdealer, photograph vendor, and real estate broker. Born 1861, Quincy, Florida. Established Jacksonville, 1876; 59 W. Bay St., Jacksonville, 1883. FU.

Storey, William F. Photog'r. Born 1879, Ill. St. Augustine, 1900. USC.

Strickland, J.H. Photog'r. Anthony Place, 1886. SBD.

Strohmeyer & Wyman. Photog'rs and publishers of stereo views. Sold negatives to Underwood & Underwood and other publishers. Took many views across America and specialized in genre subjects. NYC, 1890s. SG, Daytona, copyright, 1895; SW.

Styles, A.F. Photog'r. Burlington and Middlebury, Vt. Came to Florida for his health, in 1866, bringing with him some collodion plates preserved with tannin (dry plates). Took orders for Florida views and sent the negatives home for development, and the pictures were forwarded to his customers from his gallery in Burlington, Vt. Sold property in Vt. and bought tract of land five miles from Jacksonville on the opposite side of the river and began an orange grove. Gave up photography, c. 1871. Probably continued gallery in Vt. in his name until c. 1878 (SW). SG, dated; SW; APB (1886), p. 619.

Swift, George W. Photog'r. Born 1840, NYC. Bay St., Jacksonville, 1880. USC.

Taylor, J. Trail. Photog'r, chemist, editor, *British Journal of Photography*. Born Jan. 23, 1827, Kirkwall in the Orkneys, Great Britain; died Tavares, Florida, Nov. 8, 1895. Came to U.S. in 1879 and for a time was editor of *Photographic Times*, N.Y. Owned "picturesque" Nirthsdale estate and citrus grove, at Lane Park (near Tavares) after 1880. Occasionally lectured on photography. Was stricken with typhoid dysentery on his return trip from England in 1895 and died shortly after; buried at Lane Park. *British Journal of Photography*, Nov. 15, 1895; FU, Nov. 10, 1895.

Teahen, William. Photog'r. Born 1839, Canada. Came to Florida, 1884. St. Augustine, 1900. USC.

Thomas, Johney M. Photog'r. Born 1869, Md. Ocala, 1900. USC.

Tropical Scenery. Publisher of stereo views. SG, Mandarin, c. 1871; SG, Ocklawaha River, c. 1879.

Turton (G.W.) and Howe (E.N.). Photog'rs. Pensacola, 1889. SBD.

Turton, George W. Photog'r. Stereo views and other photography. Born Jan. 1850, Ala. Pensacola, c. 1870s; Pensacola, 1886; W. Chase St., Pensacola, 1897-1900. SW; SBD; USC; *Bliss' Quarterly*, 1897.

Underwood & Underwood. Publishers of stereo views and many other forms of photography. Founded 1880, Ottawa, Kans., by the brothers, Elmer and Bert Underwood. Bought negatives from C. Bierstadt, J.F. Jarvis, Kilburn Bros., and others. Also employed staff of photographers. Moved to NYC, 1891 (home office), and other branch offices established. Began selling news photographs to newspapers and magazines, 1896. Eventually held the largest file of photographic negatives in the world. Issued many copyrighted views of Florida, 1880-1900. The Underwood Bros. retired and company reorganized in 1931, into four independent companies. Robert Taft, *Photography and the American Scene* (1964); SG, St. Augustine, 1888, copyrighted.

Union View Co. Publishers. Rochester, N.Y. Florida Scenery, 1889. SG.

Upton, Benjamin F. Dag'typist, inventor, photog'r. Born August 3, 1818, Dixmont, Maine; died after 1899. Brunswick, Maine, as dag'typist, 1847; moved to Bath, Maine, 1851, established gallery. Invented and patented dag'type apparatus, 1853, 1854. Moved with family to St. Anthony, Minn., 1856; settled at Big Lake. Pioneer photographer of the West, specializing in landscape scenes and stereographs, views identified as "Upton." Removed to St. Augustine, Florida, 1875. Pioneer photographer of Florida who took scenic views of the state for over twenty years. In September 1898, he wrote of his work: "I am still actively at work in the landscape part of photography at 80, carting my own rig on the bike when no larger negative than 8 x 10 is wanted.... I was the pioneer landscape photographer in Minnesota more than 40 years ago, when I spent much time for 20 years among The Three Nations of Indians who were there at that time, namely, the Sioux, Chippewa and Winnebago." Still listed as landscape photographer, St. Augustine, 1899. AD; CD; BD, Me., 1855; *News Monger*, 1898; *Photographic Art Journal*, 1853, 1854; Robert Taft, *Photography and the American Scene*, 1964; St. Augustine Historical Society (prints); William Henry Upton, *Upton Family Records*, 1893; John Adams Vinton, *The Upton Memorial*, 1874; Ohio State University, Dept. Photography & Cinema.

Van Balson, A. Photog'r. Born 1841, Ala. St. Augustine, 1885. USC.

Van Bolson, Rinoldt. Photog'r. Born 1840, Ala. St. Augustine, 1880, 1885. USC.

Van Nostrand, A.G. Amateur photog'r. Member of Boston Camera Club. Displayed photograph of St. Augustine Lighthouse, April 27, 1889. APB.

Van Patten. Dag'typist, dentist. From Washington, D.C. "Daguerrotypes taken in the most perfect manner." St. Augustine, July 1843. Nsp.

Wager, S.D. Photog'r. Orlando, 1886, 1889. SBD.

Walker, John A. Photog'r. Pensacola, 1884. SW; SG, view of Pensacola.

Walker, W.F. Photog'r. Welshton (10 miles S.E. Ocala), 1889. SBD.

Watt, George K. Photog'r. Born April 1859, Scotland. Immigrated 1880. Naturalized. Fernandina, 1900. USC.

Webster & Albee. Photog'rs and publishers (some reprints), Rochester, N.Y. Published "American Scenery" including Florida views. SG; SW.

White, A.D. Photog'r. Gem Scenes, Florida view stereos. Jacksonville, 1870s. SW.

White, D.L., Jr. Dag'typist, clergyman. Took daguerreotype lessons from L.F. Fuller and L.D. Richardson in St. Augustine. "Fully competent to execution in good style. One door south of Magnolia House, St. Augustine," Dec. 23, 1847, itinerant, middle Florida counties, 1849, prices $1-$4. Instruction in the art. Sold apparatus, $75-$100. Nsp.

White, Hawley C. (and Co.). Photog'r, inventor, publisher. North Bennington, Vt. Issued many copyrighted stereo views, c. 1900-1910, including Florida. SW, Palm Beach, copyright, 1901.

Whitehead, Fred. Amateur photog'r. Life Saving Station No. 2, St. Lucie, Brevard Co., June 16, 1877 (21 miles to P.O., just north of Ft. Pierce). In letter to *Anthony's Photographic Bulletin*: "I pursue photography here under difficulties. I live right on the beach and salt spray everywhere." APB (July 1877, p. 318). Wrote letter to *Photographic Times*, December 15, 1884, from St. Augustine (1885, p. 11). An article by him on pp. 88-89,

"Dodges for Amateurs."

Whitney, N.L. & Co. Photog'r and real estate broker. Eustis, c. 1880. SG, view of Eustis residence with advertisement on rear; SW.

Whittemore, H. Dag'typist. New Orleans, 1844. Apalachicola, 1845—"Still in city taking colored miniatures." Exhibited at American Institute, N.Y., forty views of West Indies, two views of Florida, the Cotton Landing, Apalachicola, and Key West. According to the *Daguerreian Journal*, considered disposal of collection to a well-known illustrated paper in London. Traveled to South America in 1852; returned to U.S. in fall, opened gallery in New York City and engaged in making stereoscopic daguerreotypes—"The Stereoscopic likenesses and views exhibited by Whittemore at his rooms 373 Broadway....Splendid collection of West, Indians and South America. Exhibit free. Every size of daguerreotype taken." *The Day Book* (Nsp), December 3, 1852. Sold gallery in 1853. During the Crystal Palace Exhibition, NYC, in 1853, daguerreotyped works of art to aid engraver for illustrated catalog. *Humphrey's Journal* (1853, p. 89). AD; Nsps; *Daguerreian Journal* (October 15, 1851, p. 342).

Wildenhain, A.F. Art photog'r. Jacksonville, 1893, 1896, 1901. Specialized in "Mantello" cabinet size photographs and "Platino" style prints. FU.

Willoughby, Hugh L. Author, amateur photog'r. Took about forty-five 3½″ square photographs to illustrate his book, *Across the Everglades*, 1896.

Wilsey, Benjamin. Photog'r. List of views, Jacksonville, Starke, etc. APB (1886, p. 39).

Wilson, Frank. Photog'r. Born Apr. 1848, England. Immigrated 1849. Naturalized. First St., Sanford, 1900. USC.

Wilson (J.N.) & Havens (O.P.). Photog'rs. Savannah, 1874-1876. Also see individual listings. SG, Steamer Okahumpka, Ocklawaha River, 1876.

Wilson, Jerome N. Photog'r. Born 1828, N.Y. 143 Broughton St., Savannah, 1866-1880; partnership with O.P. Havens, Savannah, 1874-1876; Bull St., Savannah (Wilson only), 1880-1890s. USC; Nsp; SG.

Wise, Leonard. Photog'r. Born Germany, 1856. Immigrated 1860. Naturalized. 4th Ave., Tampa, 1900. Daughter, Annie, listed as a photographic retoucher. USC.

Wood & Bickel. Photog'rs. See individual listings. SG, view of Hibernia, c. 1878.

Wood, R.L. Photog'r. Fredenberg's Bldg., Bay St., Jacksonville, 1870(?)-1877(?); partnership with W.L. Bickel, 1878-1880s. *Florida Land Agency* brochure, 1875. Advertisement, "Old and Established Photograph Gallery." SW.

Woodall, C.Y. Photog'r. Kissimmee, 1889. SBD.

Woods, William J. Photog'r. 322 River St., Troy, N.Y. Winter gallery, Jacksonville, c. 1877. SG.

Woodward, William. Photog'r. Born 1848, Ky. Titusville, 1900. USC.

Woodward, William H. Photog'r., jeweler, postmaster. Sumterville, 1889. SBD.

Wooley, Jesse Sumner. Photog'r, lecturer. Born May 23, 1867, Wilton, N.Y.; died 1940, Ballston Spa, N.Y. Began photographic career, Saratoga, N.Y., 1880. Opened own studio, Saratoga, 1887. Associated and traveled all over America with Seneca Ray Stoddard, famous upstate N.Y. photographer in the early 1890s. Made lantern slides used in a calcium light stereopticon machine for illustrating his educational travel lectures. Made travelogue series on Florida, Jan., Feb., 1896—the first professional stereopticon lecture on Florida. Toured Europe, 1897, resulting in his famous lecture, "Under Foreign Flags," followed by the Yellowstone Park series the next year. Promoted and used the newly developed Kodak camera in the 1890s. Continued as photog'r in Ballston Spa until retirement in 1923. He was said to have been a dapper person, neat as a pin. Never wore work clothes, even when sitting on his porch, but wore a panama hat and white jacket. (Information courtesy of Bernard C. Puckhaber, joint author with Annabelle H. MacMillin, *The Grist Mill*, v. 12, no. 1, 1978.)

Zinn, J.W. Photog'r. Hawthorne, 1889. SBD.

PICTURE CREDITS

The illustrations reproduced in this book were supplied by courtesy of the following individuals and institutions. Photos not designated are reproduced from the authors' collection of Floridana.

Barber, Mike,
    (Driving a pair of prize gray mules, 37).

Cauthen, Robert E.,
    (Display counter, State Fair, 1876, 53).
    (Heiss's Curiosity Shop, Interior view, c. 1876, 65).

Florida State Photographic Archives
    (P.J. Crawford Gallery, 10).
    (Alvin Harper Studio, 11).
    (Alligator party, 1870, 26).
    (Lunch time, c. 1875, 25).
    (Welles House, 1874, 27).
    (Palafax St., Pensacola, c. 1884, 39).
    (Variety Store, Pensacola, c. 1884, 39).
    (Bicycle Club, c. 1882, 42).
    (Kentucky Club, c. 1885, 41).
    (Leon Hotel, c. 1886, 40).
    (Railroad Station, c. 1874, 45).
    (Boating on the St. Johns, c. 1874, 50).
    (Steamer *Chesapeake*, c. 1881, 54).
    (Schoolhouse and church, c. 1878, 58).
    (Spring Bath Houses, c. 1874, 60).
    (St. Johns Hotel, c. 1873, 63).
    (Wedding Day, 1876, 62).
    (First Putnam House, 1881, 63).
    (Dakin Residence, 1888, 67).
    (Afternoon Tea, 1887, 68).
    (Jessie Dakin fishing, 1888, 68).
    (Steamer *Chattahoochee*, 1888, 66).
    (A family trip, 1891, 67).
    (Kissimmee City Bank, 1886, 86).
    (Masonic excursion, 1886, 87).
    (Railroad station, Sanford, c. 1885, 87).
    (Altamonte Springs, 1886, 88).
    (South Florida RR, 1886, 88).
    (Hotel Seminole, 1886, 89).
    (Boat House, 1886, 89).
    (Hotel Launch, 1886, 90).
    (Winter Park, 1886, 90).
    ("Cracker Day," c. 1886, 91).
    (Orange County Fair, 1887, 91).
    (Lake Eustis Park picnic, c. 1885, 93).
    (Steamer Kissimmee, c. 1885, 98).
    (Sarasota Dock, 1888, 98).
    (Picnic scene, c. 1885, 99).
    (Hendry House, c. 1889, 102).
    (J.T. & K.W. RR, c. 1888, 135).
    (Anchorage, Jupiter Inlet, c. 1890, 149).
    (Steamer *Santa Lucia*, c. 1890, 150).
    (Children at play, c. 1890, 150).

Hanzl, Emerick,
    (Bicycling, c. 1882, 49).

Library of Congress
    (Unidentified spring, c. 1895, 43).
    (Boating Party, c. 1890, cover).
    (Bathing Party, c. 1890, 72).
    (Ocean Front, c. 1905, 169).

Pinellas County Historical Museum
    (Belleview Hotel, c. 1895, 106).

Puckhaber, Bernhard,
    (J.S. Wooley, c. 1903, 12).

St. Augustine Historical Society
    (George Pierron's Studio, 1887, 6).
    (Advertisement, 1891, 120).
    (Florida Club, c. 1874, 109).
    (Alcazar Pool, 1889, 121).

Pathway to the beach, Palm Beach, 1901. Photograph by H.C. White.

"Some time ago rickshaws were introduced at Palm Beach but they failed to catch the tired fancy of those who must be pleased. The present vehicle is a sort of invalid chair fitted on tricycle wheels, with a seat behind for a sturdy Negro who propels it by means of pedals." The Florida East Coast Railway booklets called the vehicles "lazybacks."

INDEX

The letter *p* following a page number indicates an illustration. See also the Biographies section preceding for additional information on photographs listed here.

A Boating Party, De Leon Springs, c. 1890. Photograph by J.A. Enseminger.

Recognized authorities on the history of pioneer photography, Floyd and Marion Rinhart have conducted numerous seminars and lectures at Ohio State University, where their important collections of early photographic images now reside. In addition, they have written a number of books and articles relating to both pioneer photography and nineteenth-century social history. The Rinharts make their home in Colbert, Georgia, spending the winter months in Fort Pierce, Florida.